VW GOLF AND DERIVATIVES

VW GOLF and derivatives
including Convertible, Jetta, Scirocco and Corrado

A collector's guide
by John Blunsden

MOTOR RACING PUBLICATIONS LTD
Unit 6, The Pilton Estate, 46 Pitlake, Croydon CR0 3RY, England

First published 1992

British Library Cataloguing in Publication Data

Blunsden, John
   V.W. Golf and Derivatives: Collector's
   Guide
   I.   Title
   629.222

ISBN 0-947981-63-2

Typeset by Ryburn Publishing Services; origination by
Ryburn Reprographics, Halifax, West Yorkshire

Printed in Great Britain by
The Amadeus Press Ltd, Huddersfield, West Yorkshire

Contents

Introduction and acknowledgements

The ultimate aim of every car manufacturer is to produce a world-beater, but few ever succeed. Way back in 1909 Henry Ford managed it with his immortal Model T and so helped to put the world on to wheels. Then three decades later Dr Ferdinand Porsche was commissioned to design another People's Car, and the result, as we all know, was the Volkswagen Beetle, sales of which were to surpass even those of the transatlantic Tin Lizzie.

The problem with success on such a grand scale is that it tends to go on for too long and then leaves a void when the glory days of the by then old-fashioned car are finally over. In the late Twenties, Ford struggled in vain to create an effective replacement for the Model T, and in the late Sixties VW went up several blind alleys in a desperate effort to find a car as widely appealing as the Beetle. Eventually, with a little help from their friends at Audi and NSU, they were pointed in the right direction and in 1974 another great success story began with the unveiling of the first Golf and Scirocco.

More than 12 million Golfs later, the success story continues with the third generation of the car, whilst simultaneously certain of the Mark 1 and Mark 2 models which are the subject of this *Collector's Guide* continue to be assembled in various plants around the world.

The original Golf, known in the United States as the Rabbit, earned lasting fame by spawning a new concept, the 'hot hatch'. Originally, it had been the intention to confine this book to cars carrying the emotive GTI label, but times change. The affluent Eighties are now history, car-related crime has led to soaring insurance premiums for some of the most desirable models, and consequently the appeal of the whole range of Golfs, Sciroccos and Jettas has been brought more sharply into focus. Hence the broadening of the text of this volume which, while still placing the main emphasis on the highest-performing and most technically advanced models, also identifies some of the more interesting mainstream versions.

As the following pages will make clear, the story of the Golf and its derivatives is a complicated one, embracing a whole mass of model designations and specification variations. Many of the cars have been specifically tailored to the needs of a particular market and therefore are likely to be different in detail from those sold elsewhere carrying the same name badge. It has also been VW's policy to introduce limited-edition models on a regular basis, which adds further confusion to an already congested model range. However, I have attempted to cover the most significant of the many model variations in an effort to underline the depth of choice which awaits the discerning used-car buyer.

Although this *Collector's Guide* is concerned strictly with cars in their standard production form, such has been their 'performance' appeal that a whole industry of conversion and accessory manufacturers has been built up around them, and for details of their products I can do no better than recommend Ian Kuah's meticulously researched and profusely illustrated book *VW Power and Style* (MRP). I would also strongly advise any enthusiastic owner of a Volkswagen to join one of the VW car clubs, regardless of whether or not the car is intended to be used in competitions. These are invariably well-run organizations which offer members value far in excess of the cost of the membership fee.

I doubt whether any *Collector's Guide* has even been written without the author enlisting help from outside experts, and in this instance I must record my thanks for the friendly and efficient collaboration of the staff at VAG (UK) Ltd at Milton Keynes, and in particular Paul Buckett and Beverley Gale of the company's public relations department, Paul Hunter, who allowed me access to the marketing department's archives, and Chris Trouse and David Bryant, who steered me in the right direction while I was researching years of photographic files.

For the final chapter on ownership I am deeply indebted to two people. I asked Richard Stephens to cast his mind back to the many years he spent selling VWs from premises in Croydon, Surrey, adjacent to where today he manages a Mercedes-Benz sales department; he responded with some invaluable advice on pre-purchase inspection and road testing which I have been able to pass on to readers. For an up-to-date assessment of the used-car market and for a comprehensive run-down on the relative merits of different VW models I am most grateful to Andy Sarssam for the time he spent with me on a busy day at GTi Specialists, of Wimbledon, in south west London, where he is sales and administration manager. Revealingly, he commented that of all the makes of 'hot hatch' which pass through his hands, he finds that VWs stand alone in terms of their enduring quality and reliability.

I hope that anyone who is encouraged by reading this book to become the owner of a Mark 1 or Mark 2 Golf, Jetta or Scirocco, or perhaps a Corrado, will be able to confirm his endorsement after finding the experience both satisfying and enjoyable.

December 1992   John Blunsden

By 1970, more than 12 million Beetles had been produced at Wolfsburg, where production was running at a rate of over a million cars a year. Here the 1200, 1300 and 1500 versions of the saloon are seen with a Karmann Cabriolet and the Coupe and Cabriolet versions of the special-bodied Karmann Ghia derivative. Collectively they comprised a difficult act to follow.

CHAPTER 1

Following the Beetle

Experiments, mistakes and solutions

Any car which has been in volume production for a quarter of a century, is still being produced at a rate of more than a million units a year and has already attracted over 12 million buyers is a difficult act to follow. No wonder, therefore, that there had been considerable head-scratching amongst the senior management and product-planning staff of Volkswagenwerke GmbH in the late Sixties over what sort of car they should produce as a successor to the Beetle.

The famous 'Bug' had been designed in the Thirties by Dr Ferdinand Porsche and developed into a supposed People's Car under the orders of Adolf Hitler, though in reality it was first to be used in various forms as a military vehicle during the Second World War. Then, after the war, it might well have changed nationality had it not been dismissed by various representatives of the Allied occupying powers who examined it and assessed it as being of little interest as a source of reparations.

So instead, the car, and the factory which produced it in Wolfsburg – the name which had only belatedly been given to the town which had grown up around it – passed into the control of the newly established German Federal Republic in 1948 and was destined to play a significant role in restoring the economy of the war-ravished country. Even when it had still been under the control of the British occupying administration, day-to-day operation of the factory had been placed in the hands of a former Opel director, Heinz Nordhoff, who had been given the post of General Manager.

The subsequent success story of the Beetle – a nickname used so widely that it was subsequently given official recognition by being registered – is, quite rightly, largely credited to Nordhoff's astute management, vision and, in particular, his decision to pursue a one-model policy built around a car whose basic design would remain unchanged, but whose detail specification would be the subject of constant improvement. When he died in 1968, he left a formidable legacy built around a car of instantly recognizable form which had earned worldwide fame for its rugged simplicity, quality of finish, impressive durability, low cost of ownership and – the limitations imposed by its technical layout notwithstanding – quite remarkable versatility. Rarely has a car deserved so richly its cult status.

Nordhoff's single-model policy, however, could not be sustained indefinitely. Despite its many virtues, the Beetle had conspicuous limitations, notably its relatively cramped accommodation and its modest luggage space, factors which could not be addressed without the abandonment of the basic shell which was central to the car's culture. Equally important, the simplicity and reliability inherent in its air-cooled engine was becoming of diminishing significance in an era when refinement, smoothness and quietness had become fundamentals of a car's sales appeal.

Efforts had been made to solve the accommodation problem through a series of larger-bodied cars with broadly similar powertrains to which it had been hoped Beetle owners would progress. This additional range, which was known internally as the Type 3, was introduced in 1961 by way of a 1500 model and ultimately became available as a 1600, with a choice of two-door or four-door saloon and three-door or

The Volkswagen 1600, referred to by the factory as the Type 3 and seen here in 1972 Fastback form, was developed from a 1500 model which had been introduced in 1961 in order to take the Beetle's air-cooled rear-mounted engine theme further upmarket.

five-door estate bodywork. As a means of broadening the total VW market it was partly successful, but the performance limitations of a rear-mounted, air-cooled, four-cylinder engine ruled out the cars as serious contenders for a significant market share in the longer term.

Unfortunately, the VW management seemed to become stuck in a groove in the mid-Sixties, otherwise, why would they have persevered yet again with the rear-mounted air-cooled engine, this time in short-stroke 1.7-litre form, for their (Type 4) 411 range, which they announced with a similar range of bodywork options in 1968 and uprated with fuel injection the following year? They seemed to be preoccupied with extending the breadth of the market for what was now an out-of-date concept instead of applying themselves to the more important task of conceiving an acceptable replacement car for the millions who hitherto had happily travelled around in their Beetles.

This needed to be a car of certainly no more, and preferably considerably less, than Beetle size overall, but with much

improved space for both passengers and luggage. As Sir Alec Issigonis had demonstrated so convincingly a decade earlier with his Mini, and subsequently with larger variations on a similar theme, front-wheel drive from a transversely mounted powertrain offered the ultimate in effective packaging.

It was NSU's merger with Audi in the late Sixties and the subsequent integration of the combined business into the Volkswagen group which was to lead to the introduction of the first front-drive VW, and the first with a water-cooled engine, in 1970. The K70, as the car was known, had begun life as an NSU design concept and was scheduled for introduction by that company in 1969 with the expectation that it might achieve a maximum production rate of around 45,000 units per year. However, in order to justify the high development expenditure already incurred, and because Volkswagen badly needed a car of modern concept, it was decided to incorporate the K70 – a medium-size four-door saloon – into the VW range, a new factory being commissioned to cope with the much higher anticipated rate of demand.

However, the K70 – which initially was offered with a choice of 75bhp and 90bhp versions of a 1,605cc single-ohc engine, augmented from 1973 with a larger-bore 1,807cc, 100bhp derivative of the more powerful of the 1.6-litre engines – was to prove a less than resounding success, and in 1974 it was quietly dropped from the VW catalogue. But at least it had broken the mould at Volkswagen, and by the time of the car's demise other front-drive models were arriving on the scene which offered considerably more potential.

In 1972, Audi had brought to market its new 80 range of attractively styled two-door and four-door saloons. They were powered by a choice of 1,297cc and 1,471cc single-ohc four-cylinder engines of brand new design which, like those in the K70, were mounted longitudinally and drove the front wheels. Then, in 1973, the Audi 80 – or Fox, as it was to be known in the United States – was followed by the VW Passat (Dasher in the USA), which comprised a range of three-door and five-door hatchbacks and five-door estates based on similar underpinnings and mechanical units.

Amongst these two ranges of cars, it seemed, were at least some of the vital ingredients for a suitable Beetle successor, and the famed Italian stylist and designer Giorgetto Giugiaro and his Ital Design studio were commissioned to produce studies for a pair of saloons and a two- or three-door coupe, the former to take the place of the various Beetle saloons and the latter to appeal to existing owners of the Beetle's more expensive Karmann-built coupe derivatives. The creation of these new designs, of which the coupe was destined to be seen slightly ahead of the saloons, would do much more than meet Volkswagen's immediate product requirements. It would lay the foundation for the development of an entirely new breed of car, one which would largely replace the traditional sportscar in the 'enthusiast' segment of the market. Without realizing it, Volkswagen and Giugiaro were about to introduce the world not only to a worthy successor to the mass-market Beetle, but also to the concept of the 'hot hatch'.

Instead of concentrating on finding a viable successor to the Beetle, VW management persisted during the late Sixties with their efforts to further broaden the range of air-cooled-engined cars. This is the 1971 411 LE, otherwise known as the Type 4, with a fuel-injected 1.7-litre engine.

VW's breakthrough to water-cooled power and front-wheel drive came in 1970 when the company adopted NSU's K70 saloon. This is a 1973 version, featuring a larger-bore 1.8-litre version of the car's original 1.6-litre power unit.

In 1973 another front-drive car, the Passat, emerged with a choice of 1.3-litre and 1.5-litre Audi-developed engines and three-door and five-door bodywork; important ingredients of the Golf were being assembled.

CHAPTER 2

Golf Mark 1

Establishment of a style

Normally, it is the mainstream saloon version of a new high-volume car range which appears first and the various lower-volume derivatives which follow later, but there were sound reasons for introducing the Scirocco – the name adopted for the coupe version of Giugiaro's new design – ahead of the two new Volkswagen saloons, which were to be given the name Golf.

One of the most important pillars of the remarkable Beetle success story had been the car's outstanding reliability, and the brand loyalty which had been built up over decades would have been seriously jeopardized if its successors had turned out to be deficient in this respect. It was therefore far better for Karmann, to whom production of the Scirocco was to be entrusted, to introduce this brand new design in relatively small numbers to enable any initial teething troubles to be identified and rectified, and for dealers to build up some service experience of the new design before Volkswagen committed itself to the high production rates which the saloon models would demand. The Scirocco, therefore, which made its public debut at the 1974 Geneva motor show, was called upon to perform a much more important function than merely replace the Beetle-based Karmann Ghia coupes. It was essentially a marketplace guinea-pig for the Golf.

But it was also a most attractive car in its own right, Giugiaro and his team having created a wedge-shaped style which was both pleasing to the eye and one which offered efficient use of parking space, thanks to its minimal rear overhang. Compared with the two-door Passat which had performed the role of a benchmark, its wheelbase was only 7cm shorter, whereas its overall length was approximately 32 to 34cm less, dependent on bumper arrangements.

Inevitably, rear passenger space was somewhat limited, but the car's practicality as a load carrier was enhanced by the fold-forward rear seat backrest and the quickly removable rear parcel shelf which otherwise was raised automatically when the tailgate was opened. Customers requiring more passenger space, meanwhile, would not have to wait more than a few months before the first of the technically similar Golf saloons appeared in the summer of 1974, the three-door version going into production during July and the five-door a month later. For these Giugiaro had chosen a two-box theme with a thick C-pillar behind the rearmost side window, a feature which would be associated with future Golfs for many years to come. Access to the luggage compartment was through a large top-hinged panel incorporating the rear window and supported by a gas strut – other than for the cheapest versions, for which a simple strap sufficed – and as with the Scirocco, the car could become a considerable load carrier with only two people on board by folding forward the rear seat backrest and, if necessary, removing the detachable parcel shelf.

Compared with the Scirocco, the Golf had more truncated front-end styling, which meant that despite sharing the same 240cm wheelbase the saloons were some 15cm shorter overall. But neither Golf nor Scirocco could have been so compactly packaged had their engines not been mounted transversely and slightly ahead of the front wheel centreline.

Three choices of power unit, all featuring a belt-driven single overhead camshaft, had been offered at the introduction of the Scirocco: the 70bhp 1,471cc engine, as fitted longitudinally to the Audi 80 and VW Passat; an 85bhp version of the same engine with a higher compression ratio, a twin-barrel carburettor and a twin-outlet exhaust manifold; and an entry-level 50bhp engine of 1,093cc with a crossflow alloy head, which had been developed by Volkswagen for an entirely different project that subsequently had been abandoned. Initially, the Golf was offered with either this engine, which was installed with a 15deg forward inclination, or the 70bhp version of the larger power unit, both examples of which were mounted with a 20deg rearward tilt.

A four-speed all-synchromesh gearbox was common to all models, with the option of VW's own three-speed automatic transmission with either of the 1,471cc engines, in each case

Transversely mounting the engine and front-drive transmission was a key factor in producing a car with acceptable accommodation within very compact overall dimensions. The Golf's luggage space could be varied between approximately 12 and 25cu ft depending on the positioning of the rear seat backrest.

The five-door 1.5-litre LS was the top Golf model on the UK market in 1975. Early cars were fitted with abbreviated front bumpers which housed the sidelights just inboard of small plastic end caps.

the drive being taken to the front wheels through unequal-length shafts fitted with constant-velocity joints at both ends.

The new cars were suspended at the front on MacPherson struts supported by wide-based wishbones and at the rear by a clever arrangement of independent suspension incorporating trailing arms, angled spring/damper units and a transverse member, pivoted at its ends on rubber bushes, which linked the trailing arms, resisted side loads and also doubled as an anti-rollbar. Steering was by rack and pinion, the geometry incorporating negative steering offset, which was aimed at reversing the tendency of the steering to pull to one side under the influence of uneven braking. The brakes were mounted outboard all round, solid discs being provided for the front wheels and drums for the rear on all models except the entry-level 50bhp Golf, which was drum-braked on all four wheels.

Both the Scirocco and Golf earned widespread praise from testers when early examples were offered for evaluation. In particular, high marks were awarded for the way in which

noise from the transversely mounted engine had been suppressed from the body structure, and for the cars' directional stability during vigorous cornering, the mild understeer being neutralized in a controllable manner during sudden power lift-off. Ride comfort was also the subject of favourable comment, as was the quality of the gearshift, something which could not always be relied upon in transverse-engined cars of the early Seventies.

On the negative side, a slight steering pull to the right when accelerating hard in the lower gears could be forgiven bearing in mind the differently angled driveshafts. The steering was generally thought to be a fraction on the low-geared side, while the brakes were no more than barely adequate in performance when subjected to some really hard use. There were mixed comments on the comfort of the front seats and in particular their backrests, and as anticipated the Scirocco's rear passenger headroom was very restricted. Overall, though, the cars emerged with flying colours from their early encounters with the specialist press, whose comments were

A desirable special-edition model, the 1983 Golf GX was based on the five-door CL, but powered by the 70bhp 1.5-litre engine linked to a 4+E economy gearbox. Distinguishing features included twin foglamps, a front spoiler from the GTI, wider wheels and tyres, sports seats and special trim.

The revised dashboard of a 1981 Golf C, on which the gear-change/fuel consumption indicator was part of a Formel E economy package which also included a 3+E gearbox, a high-compression l.l-litre engine and an enlarged front spoiler.

bound to influence the level of success these new Volkswagens would enjoy as replacements for the Beetle; the journalists' prognosis on this score was most favourable.

A choice of six models was offered when the Golf entered the UK market in October 1974; both three-door and five-door versions were available in either standard or 'L' trim with the 1,093cc engine, and the five-door was also offered as an S or LS derivative, which meant that it had the 1,471cc power unit, together with steel-belted radial-ply tyres, a brake servo and, on cars fitted with the optional automatic transmission, a brake pressure limiter. Amongst the many 'L' trim items were polished screen and window surrounds and door handles, and rubber mouldings on the waistline and tailgate. Inside the car there was a higher quality of cloth upholstery in plain colours in place of the check design on the standard model, extra instruments, door armrests, fully reclining front seats, a luggage compartment cover, the pneumatic tailgate lift, a two-speed heater blower, a cigarette lighter, a lockable glovebox and additional sound insulation. However, a heated rear

Enlarged rear light units were a visible change for the 1981 season and GL and GLS models had wider trim strips along the body sides. A 4+E gerbox became an optional extra and there was a slight improvement in rear-seat accommodation.

screen was extra, as were a laminated front screen, tinted glass and alloy wheels with 175/70SR-13 tyres.

In 1976 the big news was the introduction at the Frankfurt show of the Golf GTI with its fuel-injected 1,588cc engine (this car is described in more detail in the next chapter). Simultaneously the Golf LS was upgraded with a similar-sized but still carburettor-fed engine, the increase in cylinder bore from 76.5 to 79.5mm having raised the capacity from its former 1,471cc. However, the smaller bore was retained for a new diesel-engined Golf announced in 1977 and introduced into the UK market in April 1978, its power output being identical to and its torque fractionally greater than that of the 1,093cc petrol engine.

While the patient wait by British buyers for a right-hand-drive version of the Golf GTI was finally rewarded in 1978, another realignment of engines at this time resulted in the LS being given a new 1,457cc unit which combined the larger 79.5mm bore of the 1,588cc engine with a much shorter stroke of 73.4mm instead of 80mm. This new engine was also used for an additional Golf model, the GLS, which in addition to the current LS specification offered bronze-tinted glass, hubcaps, more substantial upholstery, colour-matched carpeting including carpet inlays in the door linings, a brushed aluminium facia, central instrument console, trip

recorder, water temperature gauge, quartz clock, rheostat instrument illumination and a padded steering wheel. A steel sliding sunroof and two halogen foglamps were listed extras. The following year the GLS was supplemented by another newcomer, the GL, which effectively was the same car visually, but with the 1,093cc engine and appropriate running gear, while the 'L' specification of the diesel-engined Golf was confirmed with the designation LD.

In 1979 the gap between the 1,093cc and 1,457cc engines was closed by the introduction of another new power unit, based on the smaller engine, but with a 75mm bore, which gave a capacity of 1,272cc, a maximum power of 60bhp (44kW) at 5,600rpm and peak torque of 70lb/ft (95Nm) at 3,500rpm. The engine proved an instant success and it led to the introduction of what was to prove a highly popular special edition of the Golf on the UK market: the three-door Golf Driver. This combined the 1.3-litre engine and four-speed manual gearbox with some of the visual features of the GTI and other high-specification Golf derivatives including the exterior side stripes, wheelarch trims and black-painted panel between the rear lights. A set of 5½J x 13in wheels with 175/70SR-13 tyres gave the car a firm footprint, and inside there was the GL dashboard and instrumentation, a centre console with clock and voltmeter, a storage shelf on the passenger's side, front door pockets, sports seats and steering wheel, black velour carpets, a 'golf ball' gear knob and an intermittent wiper facility. The model, which carried 'Golf Driver' badges on the grille and rear panel, was offered in a choice of red, orange or green paintwork, in each case with black interior.

Apart from detail variations to distinguish different models, the first significant visual change to the exterior of the original Golf took place in 1979 for the 1980 model year. Both ends of the car were cleaned up with the help of new bumpers which wrapped round the corners of the body and extended almost to the wheelarches, giving a much tidier appearance.

One year later the interior of Golfs came in for a major update, the result being improved upholstery across the range, an extensively revised facia incorporating well-laid-out instruments behind an anti-reflective panel, more generous stowage space, more effective ventilation with central as well as

The Golf Driver became another popular limited-edition model for the 1983 season. Based on the three-door Golf C, it had a 60bhp 1.3-litre engine, plastic wheelarch extensions, plus the wider wheels and tyres and, at the front, the four-light conversion also fitted to the five-door GX.

the 1,093cc engine. This comprised a high-ratio 3+E gearbox (ratios of 3.45, 1.77, 1.054 and 0.8:1 compared with the 3.45, 1.95, 1.25 and 0.89:1 of the regular four-speed 'box), a facia-mounted gearchange and consumption indicator, a large front spoiler and air deflectors on the screen pillars.

Following the success of the limited-edition Golf Driver introduced in the UK in 1980, the exercise was repeated towards the end of the life of the Mark 1 body in 1983, by which time the basic car had undergone its considerable specification improvements already outlined. There had also been a further visual change at the back of the car where wider tail-light clusters had been adopted from the 1982 season onwards, which effectively filled in the space each side of the rear number-plate housing.

Although still a 1.3-litre model, the latest Golf Driver's visual similarity with the GTI was enhanced by the adoption of a four-lamp grille with foglamps set between the headlamps; this time there were six choices of colour – white, red and blue plus metallic sand, blue and red, four of them with black and two with brown interior – and again the model was confined to the three-door bodyshell.

The five-door body, however, was adopted as the basis of another limited-edition model for the 1983 season, the Golf GX. This had the 70bhp 1,457cc engine and, like the Driver, the four-lamp front end, together with a large front spoiler, 5J x 13in steel wheels with hubcaps and 175/70SR-13 tyres, and chrome trim along the waistline, bumpers and around the glass area. Inside there were sports seats trimmed in a black/grey check, front head restraints, cloth-trimmed door panels with front pockets, full carpeting, a centre console, lockable glovebox, cigarette lighter, rev-counter, digital clock, intermittent screen wipe and automatic wash-wipe. A small number of the cars, which were offered in a choice of four metallic finishes – silver, green, grey and a colour called Llasa – were equipped with an extra-cost factory-fitted sunroof.

The last of the Mark 1 Golfs left the Wolfsburg production lines in the summer of 1983; during the nine years which had elapsed since the car's introduction nearly 6 million examples had been built and sold.

side intakes and a new range of padded steering wheels. New model designations were introduced at this point, the range now consisting of C, CL, GL and GTI versions. Apart from the badge identification, the Golf C could be recognized by its new upholstery fabrics and a better contoured rear seat, plus additional external sidelining; the CL had a polished grille surround and similarly polished trim around the screen, windows, side-impact strips and tailgate, a higher level of upholstery, a trip recorder, a digital clock, a lockable glovebox and intermittent wash/wipe; and the GL's features included luxury interior trim, hubcaps and headlamp washers. Then, late in 1981, there were further improvements to the door trim, extra instrumentation was provided on cars powered by the recently introduced 1.8-litre engine and a multi-function computer was installed at the top end of the range.

Meanwhile, the world had become economy-conscious, and in 1981 Volkswagen introduced a Formel E version into several of their car ranges, the package for the Golf, which was confined to cars powered by a high-compression version of

CHAPTER 3

Golf GTI Mark 1

Creation of the 'hot hatch'

One of the most effective ways for a car manufacturer to upstage a rival is to attract the interest of the high-performance enthusiast. No company has demonstrated this piece of marketing philosophy more convincingly than Ford of Britain during the Sixties. The Cortina was a sound product – the right car at the right time for the mainstream market – but it took two high-performance derivatives, the GT and the Lotus, to transform the company's image through successful participation in motorsport, both directly and via independent teams and private owners. The formula worked so well that on the day Ford announced its next major small car, the Escort, there was already a high-performance version, the Twin Cam, up and running.

The Beetle's popularity had been built largely through its ability to perform more utilitarian tasks than winning races or rallies, yet a whole industry of power and cosmetic conversion suppliers had been built up around its inherent versatility, and high-performance derivatives had helped in no small measure to sustain the Beetle's popularity, especially during the later years of its remarkably long life, which at the time of the launch of the Scirocco and Golf was still far from over.

Yet there was no high-performance version of either of the new Volkswagens on offer at the time of their launch, nor was one contemplated. Instead, the company's sales and marketing management was preoccupied with the task of selling models that were intended to be turned out at the rate of thousands per day. A small team of development engineers, however, felt that a great opportunity was being missed, and realizing that saloons were the production cars with the highest profile on the sporting scene, they ignored the Scirocco and addressed themselves to producing a Sport Golf.

As the project had no official backing from top management, it had to be very much an extra-curricular activity carried out in their own time, but they moved swiftly, and when they brought the result of their efforts to the attention of the Board, there was a positive response, the car's performance being judged sufficiently impressive for the go-ahead to be given for a limited production run. At this point the sales and marketing department gave their somewhat hesitant support on the strict understanding that production would be limited to 5,000 units. This was the minimum quantity necessary if the car was to be homologated for sporting purposes into Group One (Production Touring Cars) and, thought the marketing people, could be spread evenly throughout the dealer network so as not to interrupt the more important business of selling VWs to the masses.

The appendage Sport, however, was not to be adopted, perhaps because it could have proved embarrassing if the car had failed to live up to its sporting expectations. Instead, the letters GTI were chosen to identify it, a combination which has since passed into a prominent position within the motor industry's dictionary of model designations, one synonymous with high-performance appeal.

When the first GTIs arrived in dealers' showrooms, some nine months after the model had been exhibited in pre-production form at the 1975 Frankfurt show, they were greeted with as much curiosity as enthusiasm because this was very much an understated car. It was only when potential

Early Golf GTIs were only available on the UK market in left-hand-drive form, which led to brisk business for conversion specialists until RHD cars went into production at Wolfsburg in 1979.

The GTI cockpit included extra instrumentation, a three-spoke sports steering wheel, a centre console and sports seats trimmed in check-patterned cloth.

customers got behind the wheel for a test drive that curiosity turned to enthusiasm, and enthusiasm in turn to euphoria. It might have looked little different from other two-door Golf hatchbacks, but this was a distinctly 'hot' hatch, the first of an exciting new breed.

The plan for a total production run of 5,000 units was quickly abandoned as orders for the GTI poured in through the dealer showrooms, and before long cars were being turned out at the rate of 5,000 per month. Furthermore, just as Ford had discovered with their high-performance Cortinas and Escorts, they helped to increase the flow into dealerships of customers who, whilst they might not have been interested in buying a GTI, were nevertheless more than happy to become the owner of a less powerful model which, because it looked very similar to one, could bask in its reflected glory.

The engineers who had conceived the GTI knew that the basic ingredients of the Golf were of high quality and that in particular the car's basic structure was extremely rigid despite its commendably light weight. Consequently, the development

The cockpit and control layout of an early RHD Golf GTI. With the addition of a rev-counter the clock was moved to a small panel on the console which was shared with an oil temperature gauge. Note the 'golf ball' gearshift knob.

of a high-performance version of the car did not present them with any serious engineering or manufacturing difficulties.

In 1973, Audi had introduced a GT version of the 80 in which the 1,471cc engine had been bored out from 76.5 to 79.5mm to increase its capacity to 1,588cc. At the same time its breathing had been improved by fitting larger-diameter inlet valves and using Heron-type combustion chambers recessed in the piston crowns in place of the bathtub-shaped chambers of the original version of the engine. Simultaneously, gas flow had been improved with the aid of different inlet and exhaust manifolds.

This was the power unit which was to be adopted for the Golf GTI. In the first of a series of prototype cars, as in the Audi GT, the engine was fitted with a twin-choke Solex carburettor, and in this form, with a compression ratio of 9.7:1, it delivered 100bhp at 6,000rpm. However, by adapting the Bosch K-Jetronic fuel injection which had been

supplied for the Audi Fox (80) and VW Dasher (Passat) on the US market in order to meet its emissions regulations, an additional 10bhp was found for the Golf GTI before it was put into production. By this time the compression ratio had been lowered fractionally to 9.5:1, and in anticipation of the engine's high-revving ability being fully exploited by enthusiastic owners, the GTI was to be supplied with an oil cooler, accompanied by an oil temperature gauge mounted alongside a clock on a centre console. Another important addition was a rev-counter, mounted prominently within one of the two main dials on the dashboard, and because of the engine's willingness to rev so freely a cut-out, set to operate at just under 7,000rpm, was incorporated into the ignition system as a safety precaution.

Little more than the conventional upgrading and fine-tuning of the basic Golf's chassis and suspension components was found to be necessary to cope with the GTI's 57% increase in

A 1979 GTI with the neater-looking and more protective bumpers, which continued to provide the housing for the front sidelights. This car has the early style of optional alloy wheels.

power, which for the time being would continue to be fed, via a larger clutch, through a four-speed all-indirect gearbox containing the same ratios as those used for the standard Golf, although with the final-drive ratio changed from 3.9:1 to 3.7:1. An amusing little touch was the moulding of the black gearshift knob into the indented sphere of a golf ball.

Extra adhesion was obtained by replacing the standard car's 155-section tyres and 5in-rimmed wheels with the recently introduced 175/70HR-13 tyres mounted on 5½in wheel rims, while the spring rates were increased, the shock absorbers replaced by specially rated Bilstein units, and anti-rollbars fitted all round, the rear bar being mounted within the suspension's transverse torsion beam.

The regular Golf's front-mounted chin spoiler was replaced by a more substantial moulding, although no compensating aerodynamic aid was found to be necessary at the rear. The plastic covers of the extended wheelarches to shield the wider tyres provided an instant identification feature, while a large wiper for the recessed rear screen was another standard GTI feature. The standard Golf's ride height was retained for the

GTI at first, but it was not long before – in response to widespread demand – the car was lowered by 20mm, which served to improve not only its looks but also its handling. The additional engine performance also called for uprated brakes, ventilated discs being fitted at the front, and a larger vacuum servo was provided, but the standard rear drum brakes were retained – a decision which was to expose the most significant shortcoming of the car when it was driven really hard.

The most visible change inside the GTI was the fitment of a pair of rally-type front seats with substantial side bolstering and adjustable head restraints, the main cushion and backrest panels front and rear being trimmed in a bright tartan material. The front seats were widely welcomed as being much more comfortable than those of the lesser-powered Golfs, as well as more supportive when the car was being cornered vigorously. In keeping with the understated nature of the car, and in tune with its minimal use of exterior decoration, the interior was soberly finished, matt black predominating throughout the painted surfaces and extending to the trim panels, the carpeting and the three-spoke sports-style steering wheel. The fully carpeted floor, coupled with the inherent smoothness of the engine/transmission package, good noise insulation in the bulkhead area and a relative lack of wind noise, contributed to one of the most surprising and acceptable attributes of the GTI: remarkable quietness and refinement, even when being driven hard. Such standards are relatively commonplace in the Nineties, but were something of a revelation from a small hot hatch two decades ago.

It is one thing to achieve desirable standards of fit and finish and freedom from squeaks, rattles and other extraneous noises on pre-production prototype cars, but quite another to maintain these standards when the new car is put into high-volume production. There was certainly some inconsistency in the fit and finish of the earliest Golfs, but Volkswagen's production engineers worked swiftly to eradicate the problems, and by the time the first of the GTIs was ready to flow down the production lines at Wolfsburg the detail quality of all the Golfs had been much improved, even if it had not quite yet attained the outstanding level which had been

achieved with the Beetle, which of course was a much simpler car to construct.

In any case, the combination of eager performance, nimbleness, sure-footedness, mechanical smoothness and excellent noise suppression added up to a potent cocktail, under the influence of which owners were inclined to take a benevolent view of the car's minor shortcomings. For British buyers, though, one major drawback could not be quickly removed: when the GTI was introduced into the UK market in September 1976 it was only available with left-hand drive (a legacy of the original intention to confine production to a mere 5,000 units), although specialists such as GTI Engineering were prepared to carry out RHD conversions to a highly professional standard. It would be almost three more years before right-hand-drive GTIs would become available straight from the Wolfsburg factory, and during the intervening period the best choice for a buyer insisting on a factory-built RHD Golf was probably the LS or the higher-specification GLS, both of which, as detailed in the previous chapter, were offered with the 75bhp carburettor-equipped version of the 1,588cc

In 1982 the Mark 1 GTI was uprated with the new 1.8-litre version of the fuel-injected engine, which offered improvements in both top-end power and mid-range flexibility, and a seven-function digital computer. The nine-spoke alloy wheels were considerably more attractive than the earlier variety.

engine and, unlike the original GTI, were also available with five-door bodywork.

Following the eventual availability of right-hand steering, there were just two major developments during the production life of the Mark 1 GTI. The first was the 1980 introduction of a five-speed gearbox, accompanied by a change in final-drive ratio to 3.9:1, and the second – three years later – was the announcement of a substantially changed engine with a displacement of 1,781cc which, whilst it offered only a modest 2bhp increase in peak power over the discarded 1,588cc engine, gave a substantial improvement in low and mid-range torque, thereby enhancing even further the GTI's driver appeal.

A five-speed transmission had become available in 1979 on lesser-powered Golfs in the USA, but this offered the same set of gear ratios as in the four-speed gearbox (3.45, 1.94, either 1.29 or 1.37 depending on model, and 0.97:1), supplemented by a 0.76:1 fifth ratio, and was accompanied by 4.17:1 final-

drive gears. Fortunately, the GTI was provided with a closer set of ratios (3.45, 2.118, 1.444, 1.129 and 0.912:1), although the 3.17:1 reverse gear was common to both boxes. In the UK, the five-speed transmission also coincided with a cosmetic change to the GTI, for which alloy wheels of a new and much more attractive design than that of the former optional alloys became part of the car's standard equipment.

Having effectively created the hot hatch concept and stimulated a huge potential market for such cars, particularly amongst affluent younger buyers, Volkswagen found itself operating in an increasingly congested segment of the market in the late Seventies as, one by one, rival manufacturers rushed their own GTi-style cars into the showrooms. The VW was firmly established as the market leader, but it was already clear that the hot hatch was here to stay and that sooner or later one of the younger rival products would be providing a formidable challenge to its number-one status.

The Golf's compact dimensions, which had been one of its

Extensive revisions were made to the interior of the Mark 1 Golf for the 1981 season including new upholstery and trim and a much improved facia incorporating additional air intakes and clearer instruments ahead of a new four-spoke steering wheel.

widely applauded features at the time of its launch, was beginning to become something of an embarrassment in the face of roomier rivals, but the solution to that particular problem would have to await a complete reskinning of the car and its relaunch in Mark 2 form. In the meantime, an engine development programme, intended primarily for the next range of cars, was well under way and would give a new lease of life to the existing Golf range. The result was to be an engine which would not only provide an even greater level of refinement, especially in the higher speed range, but would also offer better low-speed flexibility and acceleration, as well as cleaner combustion, an ever more important characteristic in the face of the increasingly stringent control of exhaust emissions.

The 1,781cc engine, therefore, was much more than a '1600' bored out from 79.5 to 81mm and increased in stroke from 80 to 86.4mm. The need for a new crankshaft provided the opportunity to improve its balance and to fit a torsional vibration damper. At the same time pistons, connecting rods and other moving components were lightened, while a further small increase in valve diameter was made possible by the larger cylinder bore and combustion chamber, the latter now being only partly shaped in the piston crown and partly cut out of the head itself, whereas the 1600 head had been flat-faced and the combustion bowl cut entirely out of the piston. The revised head design had allowed the compression ratio to be increased to 10:1. As the emphasis was to be on improving mid-range torque rather than top-end power, slightly 'softer' valve timing was adopted with the result that peak torque (109lb/ft, up from 101lb/ft) was achieved at 3,500rpm instead of 5,000rpm, and maximum power (112bhp instead of 110bhp) was delivered at 5,800rpm rather than 6,200rpm.

The new engine was ready for installation in the Golf GTI in 1982 and was warmly welcomed. Translated into road performance, the extensive changes had given the car brisker acceleration and fractionally more top-end speed at the same time as making it more economical and quieter-running. The 1,588cc engine's appetite for high revs – one of its most endearing features – had to a large extent been retained in the 1,781cc version and could still be enjoyed whenever the mood demanded, but the improved low-speed flexibility meant that the GTI was now more than ever a dual-personality car, one which could be switched from 'open road' to 'high street' mode and enjoyed equally in either environment. By 1982 it was no longer the latest shape in town, but that didn't stop it from being great fun to drive.

Although six years old at the time of the larger engine's introduction, and with a further two years of production life to come, the GTI had undergone relatively few changes of specification other than the important ones already mentioned. The earliest cars had slim bumpers front and rear which terminated in small end caps, but as with other models in the Golf range, late in 1978 these were dispensed with and replaced by much more substantial bumpers which extended around the corners of the car as far as the wheelarches. There were also some subtle variations from time to time to the colouring of the broad stripe which continued the line of the bumpers along the body sides between the arches. Then, for the 1982 season, the wider tail-light clusters were fitted at the rear, another new design of alloy wheel was introduced, this time with nine holes, and the car's A-pillars were fitted with plastic rain deflectors.

Internally, the most significant changes came in late 1980 for the 1981 season, when new upholstery was introduced with a more dignified striped trim pattern in place of the former checks, and a completely redesigned facia was provided ahead of a new four-spoke steering wheel incorporating a large central pad for crash protection. The new facia, of a more integrated design, still provided a rectangular binnacle for the main instruments, control buttons and switches, but the two main dials, previously recessed in separate tunnels, were now more attractively displayed behind a common recessed sheet of clear plastic which also made them easier to read. There was now provision for up to three small instruments instead of two in a revised centre console, although the clock formerly positioned there had been replaced by a digital display amongst the main instruments. Interior ventilation was improved with the intakes in the corners of the facia being supplemented by two more in the centre of the car immediately above the console, while much improved stowage for odds and ends was provided on the passenger's side of the facia.

The final season of the Mark 1 GTI was marked by a special-edition model featuring a four-lamp grille, tinted glass, a steel sliding sunroof and Pirelli-styled alloy wheels.

There were alterations to the door trim panels in 1982, when combined armrests/door pulls were fitted and pockets were provided with small oval grilles for speakers. At the introduction of the 1800 engine a temperature gauge was added to the instrument panel and, beneath it, a multi-function speed, distance and fuel consumption computer, which was activated from a stalk extending from the steering column.

Throughout the world, interest in the original Golf GTI was to remain high to the end, stimulated by subtle variations in some markets and by one or two limited-production models in others. Five-door versions of the GTI were offered on the continent of Europe with the 1,588cc or the 1,781cc engine, but these cars were never made available in either the UK or in North America. As previously mentioned, from 1980 British customers were offered a special-edition Golf Driver, which at a quick glance could be mistaken for a GTI, but in fact was a Golf 1300 beneath the skin of the fuel-injection version.

Very much the genuine article, though, was the three-door Campaign Golf GTI, another limited-edition model, in this instance created at Wolfsburg during the closing months of the Mark 1's production life in 1983, and featuring a four-lamp grille, foglamps being set inboard of the headlamps, a steel sliding roof and a set of Pirelli 6J x 14in alloy wheels with 185/60HR-14 tyres. The wheelarch extensions and all but the centre strip of the bumpers were colour-coded on cars sold on the Continent, but all these items remained black on cars destined for the UK, retaining one of the GTI's most recognizable features. Understandably, the Campaign GTI has become one of the most coveted of the Mark 1 Golfs in that it represents the final evolution of a design which did all that was asked of it and more. It could only be surpassed by a replacement car of the highest quality, a thought that had been preoccupying the minds of Volkswagen's design staff since the mid-Seventies, when they set about the task of conceiving a Golf Mark 2.

CHAPTER 4

Jetta Mark 1

A third box in place of a hatch

It was only relatively late in the production life of the Golf that Volkswagen saw fit to broaden the range by introducing a pair of 'three-box' saloons to run alongside the hatchback models, and it would be 1981 before the first cars would be seen in the UK. The first Jetta had come to market on the continent of Europe in the summer of 1979 and from the start it had been offered in a wide variety of specifications. Apart from the choice of two-door or four-door bodywork (of which eventually only the four-door version would be offered in the UK), there was the option of three engines: the 1,272cc, 1,457cc and fuel-injected 1,588cc units which had

long been the foundation of the Golf range; and three levels of trim: base model, L and GL. Combined with the engine options, this resulted in no fewer than eight different model designations, although by no means all of them would be taken up in every market. The Jetta base model, the L and the GL were offered with the 1.3-litre engine, but when the 1.5-litre engine was fitted the designations became S, LS and GLS, and with the 1.6-litre engine there were just two options at first, the Li and the GLi, although a CLi would be added later.

Volkswagen were not alone in identifying that despite the

The structure, layout and running gear of the Mark 1 Jetta followed closely that of the Golf apart from the addition of a third box forming the separate luggage compartment and increasing the car's overall length by approximately 15 inches.

popularity of the hatchback – because of its versatility and its efficient use of space – the traditional saloon was still favoured by many buyers, not least because of the perceived additional security of an entirely separate luggage boot and because a conventional saloon was by definition a larger car and offered a formality for business users which the hatchback could not necessarily provide.

However, although the family resemblance between Golf and Jetta was immediately apparent, the Jetta was rather more than a 'Golf with a boot', despite their almost identical mechanical specifications. The Jetta was given smoother front-end styling, with rectangular headlights blending neatly into a horizontal-bar grille, which, together with different wheel trims and decorative stripes along the body sides, helped to give the car a distinct identity. Although the Jetta shared the Golf's 240cm wheelbase, it was 380cm (15in) longer overall, the additional length being the result of adding a vast 630-litre capacity luggage compartment, some 70% more than was offered by the Golf. Model for model, a Jetta weighed some 50 to 55kg (110 to 121lb) more than the equivalent Golf, but performance against the stopwatch was broadly similar, and on occasions slightly quicker as a result of the Jetta's superior aerodynamics.

The car's lively performance, though, which put it at or near the top of its class, was in no small measure due to its low overall gearing which, whilst acceptable for the Golf, was considered by some testers to be in conflict with the Jetta's intended role as a more refined family and business car. Also, Volkswagen's preoccupation with providing the maximum possible space for luggage had been at the expense of the comfort of the rear-seat passengers, for whom both head and legroom were somewhat marginal. Overall, though, the Jetta was well received, and for the most part it succeeded in achieving Volkswagen's primary objective, namely to capture

A neater grille, flanked by rectangular headlamps, and a more integrated spoiler gave the Jetta a frontal appearance distinctly different from that of the Golf. Two-door bodywork was offered from the start in Germany but was a rarity in the UK.

A relatively high rear window line contributed to the generous size of the Jetta's luggage capacity, measured by VW at 630 litres. This is the high-specification GLS version with a 1.5-litre carburettor-fed engine.

This is the installation of the 1.3-litre engine in the Jetta, showing the excellent accessibility of the battery and fluid reservoirs. Note the transverse brace across the top of the compartment.

sales from other manufacturers' products rather than from the Golf.

At the beginning of 1981, when Volkswagen announced a series of energy-saving measures under the banner of Formel E technology, the Jetta, like the Golf, became the recipient of an optional 3+E gearbox in which E (fourth) offered a cruising gear in which the engine revs typically dropped by around 1,000rpm following the change-up from third. The other Formel E equipment mirrored that of the Golf, but with the addition of a rear spoiler. The previous year, a diesel had been added to the Jetta range, using the 1,471cc engine which had long been available in the Golf, but the appeal of the diesel-powered cars was enhanced in 1981 when this engine was replaced by a 1,588cc version, resulting in a small but useful power increase from 50bhp at 5,000rpm to 54bhp at 4,800rpm.

The range on offer when the Jetta went on sale in the UK comprised the L and GL, both with a choice of the 1.3-litre

and 1.5-litre engines (an S being added when the larger engine was fitted), and the 1.6-litre LD diesel. Even in L specification, the Jetta was quite a well-equipped car, with rear foglamp and reversing lights, electric screen washers, two-speed and intermittent wipers with automatic wash-wipe, locking fuel cap, laminated screen and, on the 1.5-litre model, halogen headlamps all part of the standard equipment. An integrated front spoiler, a rubber-trimmed waistline moulding and the decorative side stripes were also standard across the range, while inside there was good-quality cloth upholstery, full carpeting, fully reclining front seats with adjustable head restraints, an anti-dazzle rear-view mirror, a padded steering wheel, seat belts all round, a trip recorder, a clock and a three-speed heater blower. With the GL there was also bronze-tinted glass, an internally adjustable driver's door mirror, large decorative wheel trims, metallic paint and a decorative strip between the tail-lights, as well as more luxurious upholstery, carpet inlays in the door trim, a centre console, a cigarette lighter, a panel light rheostat and a lockable glovebox. There was also an extensive list of options, including alloy wheels, a choice of automatic transmission or a five-speed economy gearbox for the 1.5-litre model, a sliding steel sunroof, headlamp washers and green-tinted glass.

For 1982, the L designation on the UK market was replaced by a C identification, which came with the 1.3-litre engine, the

The interior of the Jetta GL and GLS models was identical and included high-quality upholstery and trim and bronze-tinted glass.

1.5-litre version then becoming standard equipment for the CL and GL models. Elsewhere that year, when Volkswagen's fuel-injected 1,588cc engine gave way to the 1,781cc version, the Jetta CLi and GLi, which in some markets had shared the 1.6-litre engine with the Golf GTI, were withdrawn from the catalogue. However, by this time the 85bhp 1,588cc carburettor engine had been made available for the Jetta S, LS and GLS, leaving these cars as the top-performing models until the advent of the Mark 2 Jettas in January 1984, just a few weeks after the announcement of the Mark 2 Golf.

During the final season of the Mark 1, the Jetta range was simplified throughout Europe into the three specification levels C, CL and GL, all of which were obtainable in some markets with either the 1,272cc (60bhp) or the 1,457cc (70bhp) engine, but only the CL and GL with the 1,588cc (85bhp) power unit. In the UK, the intermediate engine was confined to the CL and to any GL supplied with automatic transmission, leaving the 1.6-litre engine for the manual-transmission GL. The 1.3-litre was only available with the four-speed manual gearbox, but the 1.5 and 1.6-litre engines were supplied with a closer-ratio four-speed gearbox, with the option of a 4+E 'box or, in the case of the 1.5-litre engine, the aforementioned three-speed automatic transmission. Apart from the 1.3-litre, for which they were optional, all models had 175/70SR-13 tyres on 5½J steel wheels, alloy sports wheels being another listed option.

Although the Jetta never threatened the marketing supremacy of the Golf on a global basis, it did outsell the hatchback in a few of the more specialized territories where three and five-door bodywork had little appeal. Despite its comparatively late appearance on the scene, it had carved itself a sufficient slice of the market to convince the Volkswagen management that next time around a four-door version of the replacement Golf should form an integral part of the overall design, rather than an afterthought.

Variations on a three-box theme. At the top, a 1983 Jetta GL featuring tweed upholstery, cloth door trim, headlamp washers, metallic paint and internally adjustable mirrors; centre, the original GLi with 1.6-litre fuel-injected engine; left, the 1983 limited-edition 1.3-litre LX with sunroof, wider wheels and tyres, foglamps, centre console and special upholstery all standard.

CHAPTER 5

Scirocco Marks 1 and 2

Golf performance with coupe style

The original Scirocco which made its debut at the 1974 Geneva show was offered in four versions: standard (rarely seen), L, LS and TS, the latter being most easily identified by its alloy wheels and a four-headlamp grille in place of the grille flanked by single rectangular headlamps on the lower-specification models. The standard and L versions were available with either the 50bhp 1,093cc or the 70bhp 1,471cc engine and the LS and TS with an 85bhp version of the 1,471cc engine. All three transversely mounted power units had a single belt-driven overhead camshaft and drove the front wheels through a four-speed gearbox. As with virtually all VW models, equipment levels tended to vary somewhat according to market requirements, but in general an L or LS-specification Scirocco could be expected to have a carpeted floor, a heated rear screen, a trip recorder, a cigar lighter and armrests in addition to the basic specification of reclining seats, two-speed wipers, electric washers and a clock.

Like the Golf, the Scirocco was the subject of several upgrades in specification during its period of production, and understandably most of the mechanical changes ran parallel with those made in respect of the Golf. In the autumn of 1975, for example, the 70bhp 1,471cc engine, which until

The introduction of the original Scirocco coupe preceded that of the Golf by a few months, the intention being to identify and iron-out any imperfections in Giugiaro's basically common design before being committed to the high-volume production anticipated for the hatchback. This is the 1.5-litre TS version.

The Scirocco's high-rising tailgate was supported by two pneumatic struts and a deep shelf shielded the main luggage compartment. The bumpers had longer end caps than on the Golf to give better protection of the rear quarters of the bodywork.

that time had been the largest on offer for the Scirocco, was replaced by the 75bhp 1,588cc unit, while the higher-compression (9.7:1) 85bhp version of the smaller engine, as fitted to the LS and TS models, gave way to a 1,588cc engine of similar output with different carburation but the same 8.2:1 compression of the 75bhp version.

The following year, for the first time, it was possible to buy a Scirocco which went as rapidly as its appearance suggested it should when a GTi model was added to the range, powered by the same fuel-injected 1,588cc engine as fitted to the Golf GTI. At the same time this power unit was also installed in another new version, the GLi, which featured a higher level of cockpit equipment and was the model chosen for the UK market, where total Scirocco sales in 1976 had risen to 3,149, almost double the 1,662 achieved the previous year. These

two cars were also available in some markets with the 75bhp carburettor version of the 1,588cc engine, when they were badged GT and GL, respectively. Across the range, the car's twin screen wipers were replaced by a single centrally mounted arm, and interior changes included an improved ventilation system with three-speed blower and a new three-spoke steering wheel with leather-covered rim.

Considerable changes occurred during 1977 when the Scirocco's front and rear-end styling was tidied-up in the grille and lighting areas, and neater and more substantial bumpers were integrated more successfully into the surrounding panelwork. At the same time, improvements were made to the interior, with less garish upholstery and trim and the replacement of the earlier tall front seats with their integral headrests by conventional seats with the headrests mounted separately on to them. The main mechanical development was the introduction of a shorter-stroke version of the 1,588cc engine, producing a capacity of 1,457cc and maximum power of 70bhp for the Scirocco S, LS, GT and GL as an alternative to the larger 85bhp engine. An additional high-spec version of the GL was the GLS – the latter model having replaced the TS as the top model in the UK. Its equipment included full

The Scirocco's dashboard followed closely that of the Golf, but a more attractive three-spoke sports steering wheel was provided.

The main wearing surfaces of the upholstery in early Sciroccos was trimmed in a bright tartan material. The car's long doors gave good access and front-seat accommodation was generous, but there was little space to spare at the rear.

Dual headlamps were part of the specification of all Sciroccos. This is a GLS with the early abbreviated bumpers and front spoiler and the single centrally mounted windscreen wiper.

thick-pile carpeting, high-quality velour upholstery and bronze-tinted window glass, while alloy wheels and metallic paint were also built into the standard specification.

The last significant engine change to the original Scirocco range occurred in 1979, when the standard and L models had their 1,093cc engine replaced by a larger-bore 60bhp 1,272cc unit, the new engine also becoming an alternative to the 1,457cc version for the GT. A five-speed gearbox became standard equipment on the GLi and optional on other models, and finally, as the production life of the first Scirocco was drawing to a close in 1980, a GTi model was added to the range in the UK featuring the boldly patterned sports seats and recently introduced five-speed close-ratio gearbox of the Golf GTI.

In the UK, the bulk of the Scirocco market was concentrated towards the upper end of the product range, and VAG (UK) Ltd, the importers, decided to exploit this in 1979 by introducing a high-specification limited-edition version, which was marketed as the Scirocco Storm. At first it was offered in two metallic colours, silver green or black, with black and fawn hide upholstery, respectively. Then, when the Storm was reintroduced in 1981, the colour choices for the exterior became silver blue or brown, and for the hide

This side view emphasizes the minimal rear overhang of the Scirocco bodywork and the small lip on the tailgate. This GLS features the later bumpers and the useful rear screen wiper.

The Scirocco Storm, a highly successful limited-edition model at the top of the range which was powered by the 1.6-litre injection engine and featured hide uphol-stery and trim, a substantial front spoiler and a choice of special metallic paint finishes.

upholstery blue or tan. The Storm's alloy wheels, which were borrowed from the VW Passat, and the colour-coded front spoiler, added to the distinctive appearance of what has since become a much sought after collector's car.

Scirocco 2

When the Scirocco range was rebodied in 1981, after a seven-year production run by the original design, the Mark 2 retained much of the character of the earlier cars, but with softer and aerodynamically more efficient body lines which also offered improved passenger and luggage space. The new external styling and interior treatment offered a more distinct separation of the 2+2 models from the contemporary Golf saloons, which of course at that time were still being produced in their original Mark 1 form.

Compared with the displaced Scirocco, which by the end of its production life was accounting for 4% of total Volkswagen sales, the new car was 16.5cm (6.5in) longer, 9.5cm (3.75in) of the additional length being applied in the luggage area, enabling the capacity to be increased by more than 20%. In the main cabin there was 1cm (0.4in) more headroom as well as more leg and elbow space for the driver and front passenger and, most importantly, 1.8cm (0.7in) more headroom for the occasional rear passengers. Despite the higher roofline, the absence of conventional rain channels and the careful development of the car's aerodynamic profile from its low nose through to a high-mounted tail spoiler enabled the Scirocco's Cd figure to be reduced from 0.42 to 0.38, the positioning of the spoiler also contributing to a 60% reduction in rear-end lift to 0.12. As with the previous model, the new Scirocco was to be produced at Karmann's plant in Osnabruck.

In introducing the new model, which had to be based on the chassis platform of the original Scirocco, Volkswagen used the opportunity to take the coupe further upmarket by eliminating the previous base model and beginning the range with an L-specification car. Standard equipment included a laminated screen, single rectangular halogen headlights, front and rear spoilers, plastic-sheathed bumpers, styled wheels, reversing and rear foglamps, a heated rear screen and a folding luggage space cover as well as a choice of trim materials for the upholstery.

The L, which was not part of the UK range, was offered elsewhere with the 1,272cc engine, but a car of otherwise identical specification could also be supplied with the 1,457cc unit, in which case it was given the designation LS. Next came the GL, which was available with either of these

The smooth lines of the rebodied Scirocco provided a substantial increase in glass area for rear-seat passengers. Although carrying a 'GT' badge on the B-pillar, this 1981 car was, in fact, a GTi with the 1.6-litre fuel-injected engine.

The considerably more spacious interior of the new Scirocco Mark 2 was trimmed in brightly patterned upholstery. Although the folding rear seat was a bench-type design, bolstering of the sides and centre of the backrest gave reasonable lateral support. When following a GTi there was never much doubt that the car in front was a Scirocco!

engines or the 85bhp 1,588cc version. With this model, smaller main-beam lights were integrated into the radiator grille inboard of the main broad-beam halogen headlamps, the bumpers and roof gutter trim had bright inserts, and the interior was given a colour-matched dashboard, a rev-counter, a digital clock and a sports steering wheel.

GT models, which were identified by different front-end styling incorporating four small rectangular headlamps, were offered with either the 1,457cc or the 1,588cc engine and could be instantly recognized from the rear by the legend 'Scirocco' carried at the base of the window. For these cars there was a set of height-adjustable sports seats, an oil temperature gauge and a divided rear shelf for improved access to the luggage space – although later this would be changed for the more robust one-piece shelf used for the other models – while most of the exterior decor was black-finished. The GTi was supplied to a similar equipment specification, but had the Golf GTI's familiar running gear of

The cockpit layout of a late 1982 left-hand-drive Scirocco GT, when the cars appeared with new upholstery for the 1983 season. The oil temperature gauge on the centre console was standard equipment on GT and GTi models.

The 112bhp 1.8-litre fuel-injected engine was installed in the Scirocco GTi from September 1982. This under-bonnet view accentuates the neat packaging of the engine between the suspension turrets and the considerable space between the radiator and the grille.

the 110bhp (81kW) fuel-injected engine matched to the five-speed close-ratio gearbox and the uprated suspension, including a rear anti-rollbar.

In the summer of 1982, in parallel with the Golf GTI, the Scirocco GTi underwent an engine change when the 1.6-litre injected engine was replaced by the considerably altered 81mm-bore 1.8-litre version, in which the combustion chambers were mainly in the head itself rather than fully recessed into the piston tops. Although the new engine offered only a modest 2bhp increase in power to 112bhp (82.5kW) a substantial 12% improvement in torque was available, rising from 99lb/ft (137Nm) at 5,000rpm to 111lb/ft (153Nm) at 3,500rpm, which was of considerable benefit to its fuel consumption. At about this time there was also some reclassification of model designations through the rest of the range, which now comprised a CL, GL, GT, GLi and GTi. There were also further engine changes, the 1,457cc unit being discontinued and replaced by a new 75bhp 1,595cc engine, while the 1,588cc carburettor engine gave way to the 1,781cc version producing 90bhp. At this point

The 1983 Scirocco GL, standard equipment for which included these multi-slot alloy wheels as well as metallic paint, internally adjustable door mirrors, headlamp washers and the 1.6-litre carburettor engine linked to a 4+E economy gearbox.

The luxurious hide-trimmed interior of the Scirocco Storm, brought back into the catalogue as a top-of-the-range 1.8-litre fuel-injected Mark 2 model. Tinted glass, electric windows, deep pile carpets and sunroof were part of the standard equipment.

the Scirocco returned to having twin windscreen wipers.

The success of the Scirocco Storm in its original guise encouraged VAG (UK) Ltd to repeat the exercise in 1984 with a car featuring a unique body kit supplied by Zender and incorporating a substantial rear spoiler and a set of very neat 6J x 14in alloy wheels fitted with 185/60VR-14 tyres, a combination which would later be adopted for the 16V versions of the Golf and Scirocco. This time the colour choices were a metallic blue or brown with blue or beige upholstery. Leather again predominated inside the car, including the steering wheel rim and gear knob and gaiter, complemented by luxurious carpeting throughout.

Soon, further model designations would be added at the upper end of the Scirocco range including two high-specification models, the GTX and the GTX 16V, which would replace the GTi. They were adorned with the body kit previously seen on the Storm, this again being finished in matt black for European cars, although it would be colour-coded on cars for the US market. This policy would also be adopted for all the European cars from 1987.

The 16V version, which was finally announced in June 1985 together with an equivalent model in the Golf range (although it had been expected more than a year earlier than this), was destined to become the first Volkswagen to be sold in the UK – albeit initially in left-hand-drive form only and to

special order – with the Bosch KE-Jetronic-injected 139bhp (102kW) 16-valve version of the 1.8-litre engine.

This had transformed the Scirocco into a 130mph coupe capable of accelerating from 0–60mph in around 7.6sec, despite a weight increase of some 35kg (77lb) over the GTX with the eight-valve engine; for this model, which had been on sale for over a year, the equivalent figures were 118mph and 8.3sec. Only about 7kg (15lb) of the weight increase was accounted for by the twin-cam cylinder head, the remainder coming from the larger exhaust system and changes to the running gear, including the stronger driveshafts and rear disc brakes made necessary by the increased engine performance, plus the provision of a larger 55-litre/12.1-gallon fuel tank. The upgraded suspension included an extra brace for the front wishbones as well as stiffer springs and anti-rollbars and revised settings for the shock absorbers; power-assisted steering was offered as an option on the 16V model. Larger ventilated brake discs were fitted at the front, but the rear discs were solid.

Standard equipment on the eight-valve Scirocco GTX was

The Scirocco GTL offered an interesting amalgam of performance, economy and luxury through the combination of the 1.8-litre carburettor engine, 4+E gearbox, alloy wheels, velour carpeting and a radio/cassette unit.

Further up the performance ladder, the 1986 GTX combined the 1.8-litre fuel-injected engine and five-speed sports gearbox with a Zender bodykit including a large rear window spoiler, Pirelli-styled 6J x 14in alloy wheels and 185/60-section tyres.

already comprehensive and included alloy wheels, a sliding/tilting sunroof, central locking, a trip computer, tinted glass, cloth-upholstered sports seats and velour carpet, with the opportunity for the front, rear and side body extensions to be colour-keyed when the optional metallic paint finish was specified. The 16V's specification went even further with the provision of electric windows, different-style alloy wheels, twin exhaust tailpipes, darkened rear light lenses and '16V' badges on the radiator, the rear panel and the base of the black-painted side window pillars. Inside, a leather-covered four-spoke sports steering wheel, gearshift knob and gaiter were amongst the 'quality' touches. On the UK market, the two GTX models were now at the top of a four-car Scirocco range, the other models being the GT with the 75bhp 1.6-litre engine and the 1.8-litre 90bhp GTL.

By 1986, the Scirocco GTX was arriving in the UK with Pirelli alloy wheels, green-tinted glass, a divided and folding rear seat and the larger rear spoiler which previously had only been part of the 16V version's specification. The other UK-market cars were now the steel-wheeled GT, which shared the GTX's body kit, which in this case was colour-coded (although confusingly GTs would be turned out with matt black kit in 1987, when the GTX was changed to colour-coded appendages) and the limited-edition GTS, powered by the 1.8-litre engine previously seen in the GTL, a model that

The two ends of a three-car Scirocco range for 1987. The 1.8-litre GTX 16V on the left, which was only available in the UK in LHD form to special order, was supplied with central locking, electric windows, sunroof, tinted glass and trip computer, while the GT on the right was the starter model and was powered by a 1.6-litre carburettor engine. The intermediate model was the eight-valve GTX, and all three Sciroccos were fitted with a five-speed gearbox, cloth upholstery and a stereo radio/cassette unit.

was dropped in 1987. The GTX eight-valve cars reverted to the seven-spoke alloy wheels for 1987, leaving the 15-slot alloys exclusive to the 16-valve cars, for which a new style of fabric trim was introduced, leather remaining an option.

The Scirocco range in the UK underwent considerable changes for 1988 when the 1.6-litre GT and the 1.8-litre GTX were joined by an intermediate variant, the Scala, powered by the 1.8-litre engine, but in 90bhp carburettor rather than 112bhp fuel-injected form. The interior trim was revised for all models, the GT having a new multi-colour check-patterned cloth, and the GTX a bolder sports check, while a more extensive range of exterior colours was offered. Although the GT was considered to be the base model, it was still well-equipped and carried the full body kit including the large rear spoiler, 185/60R-14 tyres, the 4+E gearbox, a four-spoke sports steering wheel, rev-counter, remote-control driver's door mirror, and foglamps to supplement the twin

rectangular halogen headlamps.

Five eight-valve engines were now on offer for the GT in different markets. The 75bhp (55kW) 1,595cc and 90bhp (66kW) 1,781cc carburettor engines were augmented by a European emissions-standard catalyst-equipped version of the smaller engine offering 72bhp (53kW), the regular 1,781cc 112bhp (82kW) fuel-injected engine, and a US-standard version of this with catalyst and lambda probe offering 95bhp (70kW) and featuring hydraulic tappets, which brought it into line with the other engines.

The Scala, which came with the five-speed sports gearbox, was identifiable by its colour-keyed bumpers, front, rear and side skirts and door mirrors and its 6J x 14in alloy wheels, which carried HR-rated tyres. Green-tinted glass was fitted and 'Scala' name badges adorned the centre pillars. Inside, the car received sports seats at the front, a leather-trimmed sports steering wheel and a superior radio/cassette player with

Distinguishing features of the 16-valve Scirocco included twin exhaust tailpipes, darkened rearlight lenses and '16V' badges on the B-pillars and tailgate.

Introduced as a limited-edition model, the Scala was to displace the GTX at the upper end of a two-model line-up during the final years of Scirocco production. This example is running on the open-hub, seven-spoke alloy wheels.

fade control. The sunroof and central locking, which had been standard on the GTX, were omitted from the Scala's specification, although these items were still available as extras, as was the split-folding rear seat backrest.

For the GTX, for which alloy wheels, green-tinted glass, an oil temperature gauge and height-adjustable sports seats remained part of the standard specification, the 112bhp engine was standardized for the UK market, but elsewhere all three options of the 1,781cc eight-valve engine listed above were provided, with the five-speed manual gearbox as standard. Also, as for the contemporary Golf GTI 16V and Jetta GTX 16V, two versions of the 16-valve engine became available for the Scirocco GT or GTX: the regular 139bhp (102kW) version with the mechanically controlled Bosch KA-Jetronic system and the 129bhp (95kW) catalyst-equipped version with mechanical/electronic KE-Jetronic injection. Both Bosch systems incorporated an overrun cut-off.

Despite the introduction of the Corrado, there was no intention of the new coupe becoming an imminent replacement for the Scirocco, which continued into 1989 with a similar model line-up, although with a narrower choice of engines. In the UK there was now just a GT with the 90bhp 1.8-litre engine and a choice of five-speed manual or automatic gearbox and a Scala i, powered by the 112bhp fuel-injected version linked to the five-speed sports gearbox. Both models now had electrically heated washer jets and further

The other remaining model, the GT II, seen here in late 1990 with optional alloy wheels, may have lacked the Scala's bodykit, but it was given colour-coded bumpers, spoilers and mirrors as well as sports seats, check-patterned upholstery and a leather-rimmed wheel for the power-steering.

improved audio equipment. Elsewhere, other than the 16V version, the GT was now available in Europe with just the 72bhp (53kW) low-pollution 1,595cc engine and the 95bhp (70kW) version of the 1,781cc engine, which also met US standards, the latter being the only engine available for the eight-valve GTX. A seven-function display covering actual time, driving time, distance, average speed, average fuel consumption, engine oil temperature and outside tempera- ture, became standard equipment on cars fitted with the larger engine. From this point on, only the catalyst-equipped version of the 16-valve engine was supplied with the 16V GT and GTX models, and the multi-valve engine was dropped completely from the Scirocco line-up in 1989.

For the 1990 model year the Scirocco range continued to be confined to just two models in the UK. The Scala, which had now replaced the GTX as the high-specification model of the range and was identified by its green-tinted glass and name badges on the centre pillars, continued to feature special colour-coded interior trim as well as colour coding of the seven-spoke alloy wheels which on previous models had been finished in black and silver. The other model was the GT II, a more fully equipped car than its entry-level predecessor. The standard specification included power- steering, a sliding/tilting sunroof, thermal tinted glass, a leather-rimmed steering wheel, height-adjustable sports front seats, sports check upholstery, a rear window wash/wipe system, darkened tail-light clusters, 'GT II' badges on the centre pillars and metallic paint. The GT II was supplied with similar steel wheels and chequered fabric trim to those of the contemporary Golf Driver. Both the Scala and GT II, which were given colour-coded bumpers, spoilers and mirror surrounds, were available with either the 95bhp (70kW) or the 129bhp (95kW) version of the fuel-injected engine. These changes effectively marked the end of the development of a deservedly popular range of 2+2 coupes, and by mid- 1992 only one Scirocco was still being listed on the UK market, the GT with the lesser-powered of the two engines previously on offer.

The Scirocco had enjoyed a good innings, the length of which had been aided considerably by the flexibility of Karmann's automated manufacturing facility, which had enabled Sciroccos, Golf Convertibles and Corrados to share the same line in a random production sequence. The last Scirocco travelled down that line in July 1992, by which time almost 800,000 Marks 1 and 2 cars had been produced. In the UK, 1982 had been the peak sales year, when over 7,000 Sciroccos were registered, and sales of over 4,000 per year were still achieved after the introduction of the Corrado. With good reason, the Scirocco, with its combination of elegance and practicality, continues to enjoy the affection of many VW enthusiasts.

CHAPTER 6

Golf Cabriolets and Convertibles

Fresh air with style on a Mark 1 theme

There are two fundamental similarities between the Scirocco and the Golf Convertible or Cabriolet (both designations have been used from time to time to distinguish different specifications): both models are built by Karmann and both are based on the original Golf floorpan. Unlike the Scirocco, though, the open-topped models have never sought to disguise their ancestry and more than 13 years after their introduction they still carry the angular body lines of the original Golf, although over the years progressive aesthetic refinements in the form of add-on fairings have tended to smooth off some of the sharper corners.

Although a prototype car had been built three years earlier, the first Golf Convertible made its public debut at the 1979 Geneva show. For most markets it was offered in just two forms: a GLI powered by the 110bhp (81kW) 1,588cc engine of the GTI saloon – but with only some of that car's uprated suspension and running gear – and a GLS with a higher level of trim and the 70bhp (52kW) 1,457cc engine of the mainstream saloon models.

In addition to the central roll-over hoop, which also provided the necessary anchorages for the seat belts and the guide channels for the door and rear three-quarter windows, substantial reinforcement of the body structure was necessary to compensate for the removal of the steel roof panel. As well as strengthening the scuttle area with an additional cross-beam behind the dashboard, sill reinforcement was provided between the wheelarches, a box-section cross-beam was added immediately behind the rear seat platform and the front-end structure was strengthened in the area of the suspension turrets, while the modifications required at the rear also resulted in a more rigidly boxed boot structure.

At the design stage, VW's engineers had to take the fundamental decision whether to opt for a hood which virtually disappeared from sight, and accept in consequence very little luggage space, or to retain a reasonable boot volume by allowing the folded top to rest above the waistline, the sacrifice in this instance being rearward visibility. The second solution was chosen, and in consequence the Convertible with the top lowered was given an appearance somewhat reminiscent of cabriolets of the Thirties.

Karmann were determined to provide Convertible buyers with as close to saloon-car snugness and freedom from rattles as possible, and produced a substantial top of multi-layer fabric construction incorporating a heated glass rear screen and then mounted it on a robust and necessarily quite complicated steel framework. A pair of pneumatic struts assisted movement of the hood and enabled the driver, having released the two catches locking the top to the windscreen, to lower it quite easily without having to leave the seat. Re-erecting the top, inevitably, was physically a little more demanding, and this operation necessitated getting out of the car.

Although much of the lowered hood rested on top of the body rather than within it, luggage space was still considerably less than in the Golf hatchbacks. However, a fold-forward rear seat enabled the area to be extended into the cockpit and the rear parcel shelf could be removed if necessary to accommodate taller items. Although publicity photographs at the time showed four laughing occupants peering out of a

The Golf Convertible in its original form, based on the Mark 1 three-door hatchback shell. Karmann carried out a comprehensive programme of body structure reinforcement to minimize shake, including converting the B-pillars into a rollover hoop. Prior to 1990 the top had to be folded and erected manually. Although the rear panel contained a window of generous size, when lowered the top interrupted rear vision considerably, a problem later overcome by a redesign of the folding arrangements.

Convertible being driven at speed, travelling in the rear was in fact not exactly a laughing matter for adults, who needed to climb aboard with care to avoid the padded roll-over hoop and then to accept some 2in less shoulder room as compared with the rear compartment of the hatchbacks. There was also a considerable amount of wind buffeting, although front seat occupants were well protected in this respect, especially when the door windows were wound up.

Compared with an equivalent three-door Golf, the Convertible was nearly 300lb or approximately 16% heavier. As two-thirds of the additional weight was being carried by the rear wheels it was no surprise that the open-top car lacked something of the saloon's handling poise and ride quality. Although VW's engineers had worked hard and done better than most to provide a stiffened body structure, there was still a certain amount of scuttle shake over rough surfaces, particularly after the top had been lowered.

Changes in the mechanical specification of the Convertible for the most part coincided with and ran parallel to those made to the equivalent three-door and five-door Golfs. These included the introduction in 1982 of the 1,781cc injection engine in place of the 1,588cc unit, and the change from the 1,457cc to the 75bhp (55kW) 1,595cc carburettor engine introduced with the Mark 2 Golf range in 1983. The following year the Convertible was also produced with the 90bhp (66kW) carburettor version of the 1,781cc engine.

Changes to the equipment, the level of which aligned with the GL saloon's, also coincided whenever practicable. Convertibles received the improved dashboard and control layout in 1981, including the lockable glovebox and additional console, and at the same time a towing bracket became part of the Convertible's standard specification. In 1983 sports-type front seats were standardized.

By 1985 the Convertible was being manufactured at the rate

of over 25,000 units per year and was being offered in the UK as a GL, the S suffix having been dropped, while the fuel-injected version now shared the GTI designation of the similarly powered 1.8-litre hatchback. Automatic transmission was an extra-cost alternative to the 4+E manual gearbox on the 1.6-litre GL, but the five-speed sports gearbox was the only transmission option on the GTI. All the open-top models now had the twin-headlamp grille as well as sports front seats, a specially shaped sports-style rear seat and full instrumentation including the rev-counter, while the top models were equipped with the seven-function dashboard display and leather upholstery was to become a popular option.

The GTI was chosen as the base model for a series of special-edition colour options which would be offered for the Convertible in the years ahead, an all-black version being the first to be added at the top end of the price list. It was followed by an all-white option, which was to prove even more popular, and by the end of 1986 this model was accounting for a third of UK sales. It was even marketed as the All-White model, and came with Alpine White bodywork, hood, front spoiler, bumpers, door mirrors and special 5½J x 13in alloy sports wheels. The paintwork theme was continued with white cloth upholstery, relieved by a series of thin black horizontal stripes, and with white leatherette sides and the cars were fitted out with green-tinted glass. Another derivative was known as the CC in which the white was extended to the alloy wheels, but the hood was trimmed in dark blue with 'CC' embossed on the covering. The sports seats were also trimmed in blue and similarly embossed, as was the matching cloth of the door and side panels. Blue velour carpeting covered the floor.

These special paint and trim offerings became very popular

An early UK-market Convertible GLi with full plastic wheelarch covers over the alloy wheels. The snug fit of the top is evident in this picture. This model shared the 1.6-litre fuel-injected engine of the Golf GTI, but not all of the hatchback's uprated suspension.

A 1983 version of the Convertible GTI, powered by the 1.8-litre injection engine and fitted with the more distinctive nine-spoke alloy wheels. The small bumper over-riders house a pair of headlamp washers.

and in 1987, in order to expand on the theme, the Convertible was offered in another special version called Quartet. This offered a choice of four exterior colours – Alpine White, Paprika Red, Helios Blue and Sapphire Grey – with colour-matched bumpers, wheelarch extensions and door mirrors, plus four types of cloth upholstery and four hood finishes, giving a total of 64 mix-and-match alternatives. The Quartet schemes were available on both the Cabriolet, the designation now adopted for the 1.6-litre carburettor-engined model, and the 1.8-litre GTI Convertible. The 4+E manual gearbox remained standard equipment on the model which was now badged as a Golf Cabriolet, with automatic transmission an option, while only the closer-ratio five-speed gearbox was available with the Convertible, which now carried just a 'Golf GTI' badge.

By this time the angular lines of the Mark 1 shell were beginning to become somewhat softened with the help of new bumpers moulded into the body lines, an integrated front spoiler and rear apron, wheelarch extensions and side sills. These were adopted in 1988 for another new derivative, the Clipper, powered by the 1.8-litre carburettor engine, which had replaced the GL as the entry model of the open-top Golf range. As all the Quartet models were based on the GTI engine specification, the Clipper was the only model available with automatic transmission.

For 1989, in addition to the Quartet colour options, the open-top cars were available in eight exterior colours with a selection of three colours for the hood and a new range of upholstery trim. Leather interior trim was still an option, and Quartet models were provided with a lower-cost part-leather

The limited-edition Convertible GTI CC, finished in Alpine White with matching alloy wheels, bumpers, front spoiler and door mirrors beneath a contrasting dark blue top. Note the four-lamp grille and the 'CC' logo on the rear quarter panel.

In 1988 the GL was replaced by the Convertible Clipper, the lines of which were softened with the aid of more rounded bumpers, wheelarch extensions and sill panels. The 1.8-litre carburettor engine provided the power.

47

A 1990 GTI and, in the background, a Clipper. An important milestone that year was the introduction of an electro-hydraulically operated top, which became standard equipment on the GTI and optional on the Clipper. Note the extent to which the side windows of the rear compartment can be lowered.

trim. Another small change to the interior was a new four-spoke sports steering wheel. Several other detail changes included the deletion of the chrome from the side rubbing strips, window surrounds and door handles, the addition of cloth inserts in the rear side panels and electric heating of the washer jets, while the centre console area was now colour-matched to the car's upholstery. The options list was extended to cover electric door windows and full leather upholstery in the same colours as the available cloth trim.

By 1990 the sustained success of the open-top Golfs had encouraged other manufacturers into this sector of the market which hitherto they had largely ignored, and VW was now facing increasing competition from cars with more up-to-date styling. But for the time being there was no question of reskinning the open Golfs, and instead VW concentrated on keeping up the pace on the equipment level. An electro-hydraulically operated hood became available for the first time, enabling the top to be lowered by pressing a switch after first releasing the securing clamps; the powered hood with its heated glass rear window became standard equipment on the former Quartet models, now referred to as just the GTI, and optional on the Clipper. The Blaupunkt audio equipment on

the GTI was changed from the Windsor to the Melbourne model and modifications were made to the door trims to permit the installation of door-mounted speakers.

Two more variations on the GTI Convertible theme were introduced during 1991: the GTI Sportline and the GTI Rivage. The former was the result of a meeting of major Volkswagen importers which had taken place in April 1990 in order to discuss the styling of Golf Convertibles, and it was at the suggestion of the British delegate that the German design team was asked to develop a model with a sports theme. The Sportline was the result, a car featuring Recaro sports seats in a black and red trim, tinted glass, special instruments with red needles and 6J x 15in alloy wheels. Two paint options were offered – Flash Red or black – with 'Sportline' decals on the rear side panels, and the cars were given a black hood.

The GTI Rivage also featured sports seats, but trimmed in Mauritius Blue cloth, the front seats being heated. This model also had tinted glass as well as electric windows, the 6J x 15in alloy wheels and a black leather-trimmed four-spoke sports steering wheel. Classic Blue metallic was the only paint colour offered, beneath an Indigo Blue hood, and 'Rivage' decals were carried on the rear side panels. At the same time

The Golf Convertible, built by Karmann and introduced in 1979, has always been based on the Mark 1 body style.

One of two more versions of the Convertible introduced in 1991, this is the GTI Sportline, which featured Recaro sports seats trimmed in black and red, 15-inch alloy wheels with low-profile tyres, special instruments and a choice of red or black paintwork beneath a black top.

The other newcomer was the GTI Rivage, offered with heated sports seats trimmed either in blue cloth or, as in this instance, leather. Other standard equipment included electric windows, different 15-inch alloy wheels and velour carpeting.

a higher-specification version of this car, carrying the somewhat cumbersome title of Golf GTI Rivage Leather, was offered in which the cloth upholstery was replaced by beige leather (also extending to the door handles, gearshift gaiter and handbrake grip). There was also a second choice of paintwork for this version – Classic Green Pearl metallic with a black hood.

Although by 1992 the Golf hatchback had progressed into its third evolution, it would be at least another year before the Cabriolet would finally emerge in a completely new guise. The necessity for this impending change had been brought about by the speed with which other manufacturers were at last responding to the initiative which Volkswagen had taken way back in the Seventies to rekindle the popularity of four-seater open-top motoring.

CHAPTER 7

Golf Mark 2

Refinement of a success story

The task facing Volkswagen's product planners and design and marketing staff in creating a successor to the original Golf range was very different from that which had led – after various false starts – to the first Golf replacing the Beetle as the heart of the company's model programme nearly a decade earlier. This time there was no question of seeking a new concept because the existing one had been immensely successful; the Golf's fundamental design strengths and its versatile model mix had earned itself a broadly based and steadily expanding international market, thanks in no small measure to the inspiring GTI, which had made such an indelible impact on the sports enthusiast scene. It was vital, therefore, that any Mark 2 should build on all the elements which had contributed to the success of the Mark 1, and above all should not cause disappointment to existing Golf owners and strain their loyalty to the marque when they came to consider their next purchase.

This meant that the new Golf should be first and foremost a refinement of the old, a car which offered clearly measurable improvements in all the parameters of performance and packaging, yet was still instantly identifiable in its new clothing as another Golf. History can now record, at the end of the Mark 2's seven-year production life at Wolfsburg (its manufacturing story will continue for a time elsewhere), that it met its design and marketing objectives comfortably during an era of increasingly powerful opposition in its various market sectors.

In shaping the new car, and following a policy of no change for change's sake, Volkswagen retained the earlier's Golf's most distinguishing feature, its broad C-panel between the trailing edge of the rearmost doors and the sides of the tailgate. That, more than any other feature of its more spacious and curvaceous body, ensured the car's continuing identity as a Golf, even if it did mean that one source of criticism of the earlier model – the blind spot intruding on rear three-quarter vision – had not been addressed.

The other fundamental requirement, if the car's market share was to be maintained, let alone increased, was to meet the comfort requirements of a world population which is forever increasing, not just numerically but also dimensionally. Thus the new car was to be packaged around a wheelbase lengthened by 7.5cm (2.95in) and tracks which were 2.3cm (0.91in) wider at the front and 5cm (1.97in) at the rear. The overall length went up by 17cm (6.7in) and the width by 5.5cm (2.2in).

Inevitably, model for model the Mark 2 was heavier than the Mark 1. The three-door GTI, for example, weighed 920kg (2,028lb) as against 840kg (1,851lb), but as a result of a drag coefficient improved by 19% from 0.42 to 0.34, the new car's top speed being fractionally faster with the same engine. The elimination of as many external projections as possible in the quest for improved aerodynamic efficiency also brought a worthwhile reduction in wind noise. Amongst the improvements made in this area, the rain gutters were integrated into the roof panel, the window glasses were brought closer to the smooth outer skin of the bodyshell, and although the front quarter-windows were retained as part of the door glasses, at least they were now flush with the door

The Golf GTI Mark 1, the car which created the 'hot hatch' label. This is a 1979 example with extended bumpers.

The Mark 1 Golf's 'three-box' companion, the Jetta, shown here in GL form, was introduced into the UK in 1981.

In plotting the lines of the Mark 2 Golf, VW's planners were determined to retain the broad C-pillar, which was such a distinctive characteristic of Giugiaro's original design. This is a five-door GL, which had the second highest of the four trim levels introduced with the new range.

The internal detail and layout of the 1.8-litre fuel-injected engine as fitted to the Mark 2 GTI. The already good mid-range torque of the engines fitted to the later Mark 1 Golf GTI had been further improved, with the peak figure being seen at 3,100 instead of 3,500rpm.

frame and surrounding panels.

The increased dimensions brought considerable accommodation benefits, including a worthwhile 30% increase in luggage space, while some clever and quite intricate moulding of a new 55-litre/12.1-gallon plastic fuel tank (replacing the 40ltr/8.8gal metal tank of the Mark 1) in order to make use of every bit of available space gave the car an exceptional fuel range. The roomier passenger cabin provided an additional 3.7cm (1.46in) between the accelerator pedal and the rear seat backrest, plus an extra 9.2cm (3.6in) of elbow room in the front compartment and 12cm (4.7in) at the rear. However, virtually all the benefit of the increased longitudinal space had been passed to the rear seat passengers, and the limited rearward travel of the driver's seat would be a source of some criticism in early tests of the new model.

Although a glance at the Mark 2 Golf's specification sheet suggested that the new car was in all major respects virtually identical to the Mark 1 beneath the skin, Volkswagen claimed to have re-examined no fewer than 5,200 individual components of the earlier car and re-assessed their performance before integrating them with the new componentry of the Mark 2. The dimensional alterations alone called for many detail changes, but the opportunity was also taken to improve the car's ride quality by giving the front suspension struts

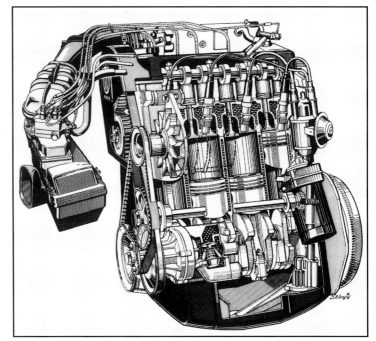

2.5cm (1in) of additional travel, while rear suspension travel was increased by 1.2cm (0.5in) to 20cm (7.9in).

Running prototypes were in action by 1981, and the extensive pre-production development programme involved almost 4 million test miles before the Golf Mark 2 was passed for production. Apart from extensive running on Volkswagen's own test track at Ehra-Lessien, many months were spent in the Arctic and in tropical regions testing in the extremes of temperature. A benefit of this work was the installation of a much improved heating and ventilation system which responded more quickly to changes in settings and the heat output of which was less dependent on road speed. The GTI and other upmarket models from the GL upwards were also provided with an additional heater outlet for the rear footwell area.

At the time of the announcement of the new range in August 1983 Volkswagen claimed that the Mark 2 had involved an investment of no less than £500 million, a significant part of which had gone into the establishment of Hall 54, a huge two-level assembly facility at Wolfsburg,

where it was connected to existing buildings by tunnels and provided a useable floor area of some 570,280sq ft. In anticipation of a significant increase in demand – wisely, as it transpired – Hall 54 had been conceived with a production capacity of 2,400 vehicles per day.

The excellent build quality of Golfs had been a major factor in their success, and with the aid of what at the time was believed to be the most versatile use of robots yet achieved in car manufacture and assembly, the factory was determined to attain even higher standards of fit and finish with the new range of cars. Particular attention was to be given to the sealing of the seams of doors and lids, and as part of the routine production process pre-heated complete bodyshells were to be immersed in liquefied wax for cavity protection in addition to receiving an underseal coating.

The Mark 2 was introduced as a five-model range extending from a somewhat spartan C model through a CL with just a small amount of bright trim, a GL with more elaborate exterior decoration and more luxurious interior trim and upholstery, to a new GLX, otherwise known in

An early Mark 2 GTI for which the Pirelli-styled alloy wheels were offered as part of the standard equipment. Note the anti-lift plate attached to the driver's side screen wiper.

Developed from the normally aspirated engine fitted to the C Diesel, the 1.6-litre 70bhp turbodiesel gave this CL-specification Golf a top speed of around 100mph and up to 50mpg.

The GLi version of the Scirocco Mark 1, Karmann's stylish coupe alternative to the Golf hatchback, seen in 1980.

The limited-edition 1984 Scirocco Storm. The coupe had been rebodied in 1981 but retained the Mark 1 chassis platform.

The 1.8-litre fuel-injected engine installed in the front of a Mark 2 GTI. Ample working space had been provided for all routine maintenance tasks.

some markets as the Carat. This had power-assisted steering, electric window lifts and central locking as part of the standard equipment, and once again there was a range-topping GTI with its 1.8-litre fuel-injected engine and this time a choice of three-door or five-door bodywork.

Standard equipment on the C model extended to cloth door and side panel trims, a rear window wash/wipe system with intermittent wipe and a rear foglamp. With the CL there was a wider choice of colours and moulded rubber strips down the body sides, front door storage bins, additional ventilation outlets in the centre of the facia and a trip distance recorder. The specification for a GL included a higher grade of material for the seats and door trims, a divided rear seat base and backrest, a centre console and a fully lined and illuminated luggage compartment. The four-door Carat, or GLX, was loaded with standard equipment including power-steering, electric window lifts, central locking, metallic paint,

electrically heated and adjusted door-mounted rear-view mirrors, velour upholstery, a leather-covered steering wheel, full instrumentation including the rev-counter and multi-function computer display and a high-quality stereo radio and cassette player system. The main identification features of the GTI were the twin-headlight grille, a larger front spoiler, the twin-tailpipe exhaust system and the fluorescent red trim-strips on the bumpers and side body mouldings.

At this stage, engine changes for the new Golf were confined to the lesser-powered models, beginning with a 55bhp (40.5kW) 1,272cc (75 x 72mm) engine replacing the earlier 1,093cc (69.5 x 72mm) base unit. Although at the bottom end of the Golf range, the 1.3-litre engine was quite a sophisticated unit featuring a two-stage carburettor, hydraulic tappets, a five-bearing camshaft and electronic ignition and it was fitted with long-life spark plugs which only required renewing every 18 to 20,000 miles. With the

The cockpit of a Mark 2 GTI. With two large central intakes supplementing those at the ends of the facia, ventilation was considerably more efficient than in the Mark 1. Note how the golf ball theme had been retained for the gearshift.

Bright contrasting horizontal stripes was the theme chosen for the Mark 2 GTI's upholstery and door trim. Note how the armrests have been neatly recessed into the door panels in order to maximize elbow room. Like the doors, the tailgate will remain open at a wide angle.

The 1989 Mark 2 Golf GTI 16V. Also available as a five-door model, the GTI was offered with the 16-valve engine from 1986.

The Jetta Mark 2, seen carrying a GTI badge on the bolder grille introduced in 1988, was much more than a 'three-box' Golf.

emphasis on economy and reduced emissions, this engine was also available with what Volkswagen called their Formel E package, which incorporated an automatic stop-start system whereby within 2sec of the car slowing to 3mph and the engine being reduced to idling speed, it would be switched off and then automatically switched on again as first, second or reverse gear was engaged.

Further up the scale, a new 75bhp (55kW) 1,595cc (81 x 77.4mm) engine was offered in place of the 1,457cc (79.5 x 73.4mm) unit from the Mark 1, and there was the addition of a 90bhp (66kW) 1,781cc (81 x 86.4mm) engine for the GLX, which was closely related to the GTI's power unit, but fed instead through a carburettor. However, a catalyst-equipped version with Bosch KE-Jetronic fuel injection and delivering a similar power output to the carburettor engine would later become available for the US market.

Whereas a four-speed gearbox continued to be standard equipment on the C, CL and GL models, a 4+E box incorporating a high-economy fifth ratio was available as part of a Formel E package, which had been introduced in different forms into various Volkswagen ranges in a mood of environment consciousness, and was standard equipment for the GLX and the newly introduced 1,588cc turbodiesel model. The GTI, of course, like its Mark 1 predecessor, would continue to benefit from a five-speed close-ratio gearbox, but now used in conjunction with a higher 3.67:1 final-drive ratio.

Unsurprisingly, most of the changes incorporated into the design of the Mark 2 were well received by the vast majority of Golf (as distinct from Golf GTI) buyers. The car's increased roominess, especially in the rear compartment, represented a major plus, as did the improved noise suppression, the increased engine performance and flexibility, and the subtle improvement over the already high standards of ride comfort and steering response achieved with the Mark 1. It was when making a direct back-to-back assessment of the new and old GTIs that enthusiasm for the newcomer was at first somewhat more muted.

Unlike the Mark 1, the replacement GTI was available from the start with five-door as well as three-door bodywork. This is a 1986 model with a deeper front spoiler than the three-door car pictured on page 55.

One of the most prolific Golfs on the UK market, this 1987 CL had a new design of tweed upholstery, velour carpeting, a stereo radio/cassette player, internally adjustable door mirrors and separate heater vents for the rear compartment.

Without doubt – and intentionally – the new bodyshell lacked the sharpness, crispness and compactness of the earlier cars', and consequently it made the new GTI even more understated as a performance car. There were suggestions by critics that Volkswagen had 'gone soft' on the Golf, that in the face of increasing competition within the now widely recognized and progressively more important hot hatch market, the German manufacturer had allowed itself to become wrong-footed by its rivals, and that cars with more visible flair would in future be setting the pace in the showrooms.

But this was an overly emotive reaction, as the ever-increasing sales of Golf GTIs would demonstrate in the years ahead. Usually it was only necessary to sit a sceptic in the driver's seat and hand over the ignition key to turn him or her into a convert. Those familiar with the Mark 1 found that despite the new car's increased weight, acceleration was at least or almost as brisk up to most motorway speed limits, and that although it tailed off slightly towards the 80mph mark, the improved aerodynamics of the new car then came to its aid at the top end of speed range, where it was

significantly quicker than the earlier model.

At least as important, low-speed flexibility seemed even better and, for drivers of right-hand-drive cars in particular, the all-disc brake system provided a much more assuring pedal feel now that the cross-linkage, which had been necessary in the conversion of the Mark 1's LHD layout, had been eliminated. The noise level in the cockpit had been reduced substantially, and the Mark 1's slightly metallic-sounding exhaust note had been replaced by a much lower-pitched sound, which only became obtrusive towards the top end of the speed range, well beyond the cruising revs in fifth gear.

One of the most important landmarks in the Mark 2 GTI's history occurred for the 1986 model year with the introduction of the 139bhp (102kW) 16-valve twin-ohc version of the 1.8-litre engine, which provided a new performance flagship for the Golf range, the GTI 16V, although the first examples of the multi-valve-engined car were destined not to reach the UK until October 1986, several months after the new engine had been available (to special order only) in the Scirocco. A full description of the 16-valve engine will be found in the next chapter.

The Corrado 16V, introduced in 1989, was intended to move VW into the sportscar market rather than replace the Scirocco.

By the mid-Eighties the wave of ecological consciousness which had started in California and gradually extended to other parts of the United States was also becoming an urgent matter in Europe – especially so in Germany – and it was clear that car manufacturers could ignore this trend at their peril. Volkswagen was already at the sharp end of the drive to produce 'cleaner' cars, and by 1985 both the eight-valve and the 16-valve versions of the GTI's engine were being manufactured with full emissions-control equipment incorporating a catalyst and a lambda probe in the exhaust system (the latter being connected to an electronic unit for accurate mixture control), these engines being available for sale in Europe as well as in the USA.

With the GTI's eight-valve engine, on which the fuel mixture was fed from a mechanical/electronic Bosch KE-Jetronic injection system, the effect of the emissions-control equipment was to reduce the maximum power output by 5bhp to 107bhp (79kW) at 5,250rpm and peak torque by just 3lb/ft to 111lb/ft (154Nm) at 3,250rpm, while for the 16-valve engine with KE-Jetronic injection and similar emissions-control equipment the power figure came down by 10bhp to 129bhp (95kW) at 5,800rpm although the maximum torque remained at just under 122lb/ft (168Nm), but at the lower speed of 4,250 instead of 4,600rpm. The 16-valve engine in this form, being equipped with a knock-sensing device, could be run on regular-grade unleaded fuel.

On its introduction the Golf GTI 16V could be distinguished from an eight-valve GTI in several ways. Although only the most perceptive eye was likely to detect that the 16V sat 1cm (0.4in) lower and had stiffer springs, dampers and anti-rollbars, the fluorescent red '16V' emblems on the body immediately identified the car, the motif being repeated inside on the glovebox flap. Another recognition point was the use of 185/60VR-14 tyres on 6in wide steel wheel rims in place of the HR-rated tyres used when the eight-valve engine was fitted. The 16V's spring stiffness was increased by 10% at the front and 20% at the rear, and modified shock absorbers were fitted, providing improved damping on the rebound stroke. The diameter of the ventilated front brake discs was increased by 17mm to 256mm, larger brake pistons were provided all round and air

Three of many options offered in 1987. Top, the Golf Driver with quad headlamps, wider steel wheels and black wheelarch extensions; centre, the limited-edition Golf Tour featuring special upholstery, metallic paint and the 1.8-litre carburettor engine; bottom, a GTI with the latest 'tear drop' alloy wheels.

65

A 1988 Golf Driver featuring the body changes which had been introduced late the previous year. These included the revised grille, the elimination of the quarterlights from the front doors and the repositioning further forward of the door mirrors, and revisions to the bumpers and side mouldings. Another much-welcomed improvement was a pair of wipers that now parked to the left on RHD cars, greatly assisting wet-weather visibility.

ducts were let into the front spoiler to assist brake cooling. This was very much a high-specification model, and there was a roof-mounted radio aerial with an electronic amplifier, tinted glass and central locking as well as all the regular items listed for the eight-valve GTI, which included the twin-headlight grille, wheelarch extensions, rear spoiler, twin exhaust tailpipes, sunroof, multi-function dashboard display and rev-counter and sports seats.

Minor improvements throughout the Golf range were made to the 1987 cars, all of which had a height-adjustable driver's seat and similarly adjustable top seat belt mounts, while the CL received the cloth upholstery, velour carpeting and padded steering wheel from the previous year's GL, together with internally adjustable rear-view mirrors, a full centre console, heater vents for the rear footwells and a soft padded gearshift knob. Automatic transmission was introduced as an option on petrol-engined CLs.

The GL model, for which automatic transmission was also an option, was taken a step further upmarket with new striped tweed velour upholstery, tinted glass, the GTI's four-spoke sports steering wheel, the padded gear knob and wider rubbing strips on the body sides. Stereo radio/cassette units were now standard across the range in the UK, where the Golf C became available with five-door bodywork for the first time. An important improvement to visibility was the deletion of the quarter-windows from the doors and the relocation further forward of the rear-view mirrors. The only change specific to the GTI, apart from the introduction of the 16-valve version alongside the eight-valve model, was an alteration to the style of the alloy wheels, which remained standard with five-door bodywork, but an optional extra for three-door cars.

The Driver model designation, which had been used to identify a limited-edition version of the original Golf and latterly for a similar exercise with the Golf 2, was brought into the main catalogue during 1987 for a model which combined much of the external identity of a GTI with the 1.6-litre carburettor-equipped engine. The 'Driver' badge, which adorned the grille of both three-door and five-door bodies, was accompanied by quadruple halogen headlamps, tinted glass, black wheelarch extensions and body sills, 6J x 14in rally-style steel wheels and low-profile tyres, the cars being trimmed internally in a grey-blue check cloth and fitted with a sports steering wheel.

More extensive changes were made to the Golf saloon range for 1988, the most visible being the replacement of the familiar seven-slot radiator grille by a new and bolder five-slot design with an enlarged VW badge in the centre of it. The badging at the rear was also changed, the Volkswagen name on the left being deleted and replaced by a centrally placed circular VW badge with the model designation in a more

dynamic script on the right side of the panel. The wider side rubbing strips between the wheelarches were extended to the base model, as were the centre air vents in the dashboard, and all Golf models received a new steering wheel, twin-jet screen washers and redesigned steering column stalk switches. Larger door bins were provided for the CL and higher-specification models and additional choices of paint finish were provided at the top of the range. Standard GL equipment now included the twin electrically controlled and heated mirrors and central locking of the doors, boot and fuel filler cap. For the GTI models, the interior improvements included new cloth trim.

The 16-valve version of the GTI continued to be identified by the bright red '16V' plates beneath the GTI badges, air ducting to the front spoiler and the electric roof-mounted aerial. A digital instrument pack was offered as an optional

Although five-door GTIs continued to be supplied in the UK with alloy wheels in 1989, they were optional on three-door cars, for which these 6J steel wheels were standard equipment.

alternative to the standard arrangement of dials, but it was not well received so was quietly forgotten. An additional GT model was available in certain markets, equipped with the GTI's running gear, but powered by either a 90bhp (66kW) version of the 1,781cc engine with mechanical fuel injection and catalyst, or an 84bhp (62kW) carburettor-equipped version of the same engine. These cars featured the twin-headlight grille, black sill and wheelarch extensions, sports steering wheel, rev-counter and multi-function dashboard display, and were available optionally with ABS brakes. A similar twin-headlight grille, bodywork extensions and special interior equipment was offered on the Golf GTD, a sports-oriented Golf powered by the turbocharged diesel engine.

Only minor refinements were made to the mainstream models for the 1989 season when Volkswagen's big news was the announcement of the Corrado, which is discussed in a later chapter. The storage bins on the front doors were now part of the standard equipment of all Golfs, as were electrically heated washer jets and a new wide-angle mirror for the driver's door. The CL models now had twin headlamps and

were identified by silver-coloured hubcaps, and the GLs were provided with a new range of high-grade velour upholstery and trim. For the GTI models, the main distinguishing feature was another new design of alloy wheel, this time with seven large slots in place of the previous 15 smaller openings around the periphery. The new Syncro model, featuring permanent four-wheel drive and incorporating a viscous coupling, was to be based on the five-door CL package, but with the 1.8-litre carburettor engine, five-speed sports gearbox, black wheelarch extensions, 6J x 14in steel wheels, low-profile tyres, twin headlamps, central locking and, inside the car, a sports steering wheel, split folding rear seat, rev-counter and power-assisted steering. However, within a year the Syncro would revert to the standard CL package.

There was a more visible upgrade for the 1990 Golfs, most notably the new and more integrated bumper and apron mouldings front and rear for the GL and GTI and revisions to the front foglamps and to the side rubbing strips, while the GTI 16V gained BBS 6J x 15in wheels, 185/55R-15 tyres and power-steering as part of its standard specification, although

The well-equipped five-door GL, which in 1989 received new velour upholstery and trim, while all Golfs were supplied with electrically heated washer jets and a wide-angle mirror for the driver's door.

The Golf Ryder, seen here in 1990, began life as a high-specification five-door car powered by the economy 1.3-litre carburettor engine, although for 1992, the Mark 2's final season, it would be upgraded to the 1.6-litre engine. The sunroof, four-headlamp grille and special upholstery were all part of the standard equipment.

central locking and electric front windows became options. The 16V was also given darkened rear light clusters and the special upholstery previously confined to a limited-edition version. A more environmentally friendly 1.6-litre catalyst-equipped turbocharged diesel engine was introduced in place of the earlier unit, and most Golfs were available with new colour and upholstery combinations, black becoming the standard for the interior trim. Central locking became part of the CL and GL specification, the CL also receiving new wheel trims. The GL also received a sports steering wheel. At the same time there were also some deletions, the GL losing the chrome trim applied to the earlier bumpers, while the GTI lost the red strip previously seen on the bumpers and side mouldings. The 1990 season also marked the introduction of an intriguing newcomer at the top of the GTI

range, the supercharged G60, which is described in the next chapter.

Although the long-rumoured Golf 3 was destined to be announced during 1991, the Mark 2 was still far from being a spent force and the range was wider than ever in its final season. There were no fewer than seven engine options across different markets for the CL and GL three-door and five-door models – 1.3, 1.6 and 1.8-litre petrol engines and four 1.6-litre diesels, two of them turbos, of which one had charge air cooling. The GT, available in both body styles, marked the start of the 1.8-litre engine range, followed by the GTI in both eight-valve and 16-valve forms and the supercharged G60. The GT-specification cars were also available as 1.6-litre GTD turbodiesels, with or without charge air cooling, and there were still CL and GT versions of the four-wheel-drive Syncro in both body styles, and a logical development of these cars, the Golf Country, with raised bodywork and long-travel suspension tailored to off-road use.

Understandably, only minor changes in specification were made to the mainstream models for their final season of production at Wolfsburg; they included the option of part-leather interior trim and further choices of alloy wheels as well as a final modification to the front-end lower panelling to accommodate the integrated foglamps. In the UK, the Golf hatchback range was slimmed down to just five models for the 1992 season pending the arrival of the Golf 3. Inevitably, two of the cars were the GTI in eight-valve and 16-valve

A smart LHD three-door Golf GL in 1989 guise, complete with optional 'tear drop' alloy wheels and matt black door mirrors matching the body side mouldings and bumpers.

The same bodyshell, but this is a 1990 CL, the main visible differences being the lack of bright trim strips on the bumpers, windscreen and side window frames and, of course, the plastic-covered steel wheels.

By 1990 Volkswagen were making much of the environmental cleanliness of their 1.6-litre diesel-engined cars as well as their economy. This is the Golf CL Umwelt Diesel.

As well as offering their normally aspirated diesel engine with a catalyst prior to the 1990 season, VW introduced this second version of their turbodiesel with additional charge air cooling for both the Golf and Jetta, which were given the GTD designation.

Another Golf Driver, this time with three-door bodywork, in its final 1992 specification with 1.8-litre engine in place of the previous 1.6-litre unit. The extra performance, coupled with the Driver's high level of standard equipment, made it a deservedly popular model in the Mark 2's final season.

forms, and they were accompanied by just three special-edition cars, beginning with the Ryder, the previous 1.3-litre engine of which was replaced by the 75bhp 1.6-litre power unit, which was accompanied by a five-speed gearbox and wider wheels and tyres. The Ryder also came with a sunroof, special upholstery, the twin-headlamp GTI-style front end and, of course, special badging.

The Driver, previously a 1.6-litre car, became a 1.8-litre model with the 90bhp carburettor engine, with the option of automatic transmission in place of the five-speed manual gearbox. Central locking, sunroof, tinted glass, low-profile tyres, split folding rear seats, a tachometer and the twin-headlamp grille were all part of the standard specification.

Like the GTI and Ryder, the Driver was available in both three-door and five-door bodywork, whereas the remaining model, the 1.6-litre 80bhp turbocharged diesel-engined GTD, was offered in five-door form only with the manual gearbox.

By the time these final Mark 2 models had gone on sale, well in excess of 12 million Golfs of the two series had been produced, of which more than a million were GTIs. Rather like the Beetle before it, the enduring familiarity of the Golf's shape, the essential elements of which had been carried over from the Mark 1 to the Mark 2, had helped to reinforce the public's enthusiasm for the car and to earn it the status of both trendsetter and classic of its time.

CHAPTER 8

The high-tech Golfs

16V, Syncro, Rallye and G60

Three major technical developments, all of which were announced over a period of a few months following the summer of 1985, were to have a major impact on the expansion of the Golf range and that of its derivatives during the years ahead. The first was the announcement of a 16-valve version of the GTI's 1,781cc fuel-injected engine, the second was the introduction of Volkswagen's Syncro transmission system, which enabled the Golf to become the first standard production car in the compact class to feature permanent four-wheel drive, and the third was the unveiling of the company's G-lader, or mechanically driven supercharger. The latter was first coupled to the 1,272cc engine to create a new model at the top end of the Polo range, the G40, but it was soon to be featured in the Golf product line-up by being used in conjunction with the eight-valve 1,781cc engine. The resulting car, the Golf G60, was the volume-production derivative of a limited-production model, the Rallye Golf, a 5,000-unit 'homologation special' which had been produced during 1989 primarily for competition purposes.

The 1,781cc 16-valve engine
By the summer of 1985, when the 16-valve version was announced, Volkswagen's eight-valve EA 827 engine was already firmly established as one of the classic four-cylinder designs of the modern era, some 5 million petrol-consuming or diesel examples having been built from the time it made its debut in the Audi 80 in 1972. The following year the Passat had become the first Volkswagen to adopt it, but inevitably it was the introduction of the Golf range in 1974 which had

accelerated its success, and the arrival of the GTI two years later and its subsequent successful and versatile competition career which had unlocked the engine's high-performance potential.

Competition-tuned engines had performed reliably when delivering specific outputs in excess of 100bhp (75kW) per

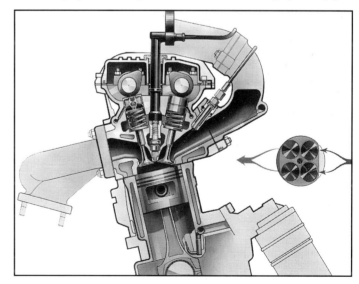

Drawing of a section through the 16-valve cylinder head, in which the exhaust valves are positioned vertically and the inlets at an angle of 25deg. The piston crowns are cooled by oil jets from the main oilway.

litre, despite the intake breathing restriction imposed by having only one inlet and one exhaust valve per cylinder, so the potential of the engine when fitted with a multi-valve cylinder-head was too promising to ignore.

But use in competitions was insufficient justification on its own for the high development costs involved in producing such

A display model of the 16-valve engine. The toothed belt drives the exhaust camshaft, from which the inlet camshaft is driven at the other end of the engine by a short chain and sprockets.

an engine, and when work began on the project in November 1981 the brief was to produce a power unit which would not only deliver a higher output than the current eight-valve fuel-injected engine, but would do so whilst at least matching and if possible improving upon its specific fuel consumption. Further developing the theme which had been adopted when the 1.6-litre petrol engine had been superseded by the bigger-bore 1.8-litre version, the proposed 16-valve was to be a high-torque unit, thereby offering customers at the top end of the Golf's market spectrum a higher level of refinement as well as of outright performance than existing models could offer.

In place of the conventional head, with its set of four single 40mm inlet valves and four single 33mm exhaust valves operated from a single belt-driven overhead camshaft, the thermally hardened cast-alloy 16-valve head was to have two chain-connected counter-rotating camshafts, one moving pairs of 32mm diameter inlet valves and the other the dual 28mm exhaust valves. This layout offered an improvement in gas flow of more than 20%. The centrally located spark plugs ensured a short flame path for the combustion mixture and optimum filling of the chambers. An unusually narrow angle of 25deg between the two lines of valves meant that the engine width across the camshaft housings could be kept relatively narrow.

The use of a special hardened steel for the inlet valves and sodium filling of the exhaust valve stems was good news for those interested in the engine's competition potential, while the adoption of hydraulic bucket tappets in order to reduce both servicing costs and mechanical noise was an interesting development for an engine with such high-performance pretensions. The extra oil supply required by the hydraulic tappets was provided by borrowing the oil pump from the diesel version of the eight-valve engine, which offered a 15% higher throughput, and oil jets from the main oil gallery in the cylinder block helped to cool the underside of the piston crowns.

A compression ratio of 10:1 was adopted for the 16-valve engine, fuel being supplied by the mechanically controlled Bosch KA-Jetronic injection system incorporating idle-speed filling control and an overrun fuel cut-out. Maximum power output showed a 24% increase on the eight-valve engine's

When the 16-valve engine was announced in 1985 it was offered in both the three-door version of the Golf GTI and the Scirocco GTX. In addition to the badging, cars with the multi-valve engine could be identified by these 15-slot alloy wheels.

No doubt about which engine is in the front of this GTI. Presumably the glovebox lid was chosen for the '16V' badge in order to impress the passenger!

Cars with the 16V engine rode lower and were fitted with uprated springs, dampers and anti-rollbars, the spring stiffness at the rear being increased by 20%. Larger pistons were fitted to the disc brakes.

figures at 139bhp (102kW) at 6,300rpm and the engine would continue to rev willingly up to 7,000rpm. At first, a peak torque of 116lb/ft (160Nm) was claimed at 4,500rpm, although the figures were subsequently amended to 121.5lb/ft (168Nm) at 4,600rpm, but of more significance was the fact that the torque curve was almost flat from 4,000 to 6,000rpm and respectable pulling power was available from around 2,500rpm. There was, of course, a price to pay for this increased performance, and when the Golf GTI 16V first went on sale in the UK it was considerably more expensive than the existing model with the eight-valve engine.

When fitted with emissions-control equipment, which included a knock-sensing device enabling it to run on regular-grade unleaded fuel, there was inevitably a loss of top-end power, but the 16-valve engine was still a vigorous performer and could produce a peak figure of 129bhp (95kW) at 5,800rpm, while maximum torque was virtually unchanged at 121lb/ft (168Nm), and achieved at the slightly lower crankshaft speed of 4,250rpm. By way of comparison, the

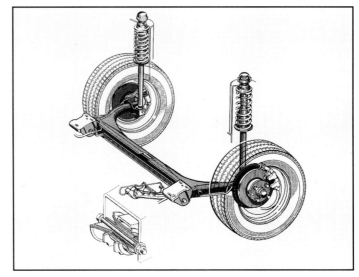

This new design of seven-slot alloy wheel was offered with a special-equipment version of the GTI 16V in 1988, by which time total production of all Golfs had passed the 10 million mark

By 1990 a much more integrated rear bumper and apron had helped to smooth the lines of the high-performance Golf, with just the small recesses on the left side to accommodate the twin tailpipes of the 16V engine. During that year cars in the UK could also be supplied with the optional BBS multispoke alloy wheels seen on the car to the right.

GTI's eight-valve engine, on which the fuel mixture was fed from a mechanical/electronic Bosch KE-Jetronic injection system, the effect of the emissions-control equipment was to reduce the maximum power output to 107bhp (79kW) at 5,250rpm with peak torque of 111lb/ft (154Nm) at 3,250rpm.

Syncro four-wheel drive
At the time of introduction in February 1986, Volkswagen went to considerable lengths to justify the sophistication of their Syncro system of permanent four-wheel drive against the relative simplicity of selectable 4WD. The latter, they maintained, acted primarily as a traction aid on slippery surfaces and generally at low speed, and moreover such

systems were difficult to combine with ABS braking. Permanent 4WD offered two solutions, one with fixed power distribution and the other (which was chosen for Syncro) with slip-sensitive power distribution, achieved by replacing the centre differential and controlling the distribution by a viscous coupling integrated into the drive train.

The viscous coupling in the Syncro system is contained within a drum-shaped housing of approximately 6in diameter bolted to the propshaft, with a further driveshaft connecting it to the rear axle differential. The housing contains 59 closely spaced steel plates, 30 of which have holes bored in them and are fixed to the housing. The other 29 slotted plates are fixed to a driveshaft connected to the rear differential. There is no direct connection between the two types of plates, power

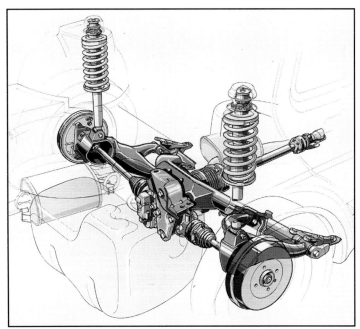

The rear-drive layout of the Golf Syncro with the viscous coupling mounted on the rear of the propshaft, just forward of the differential gears.

The front-drive arrangements for the Syncro were little changed from normal other than the need for differently rated springs and dampers.

From this view discreet badges on the grille and just forward of the leading door identify this as a Golf with permanent four-wheel drive. The large front spoiler and extended wheelarches were standardized on this model.

The Syncro was based on the CL-specification Golf but with a few refinements such as the four-spoke sports steering wheel, padded dashboard and centre console. A split rear seat was also provided to compensate for the reduced luggage space resulting from the rear transmission.

A 1988 UK-market Syncro featuring the four-headlamp grille but just the unadorned steel wheels.

transmission being effected by a highly viscous silicon oil which offers special visco-elastic properties in high-temperature conditions.

Small differences in the rotational speed of front and rear wheels, and thus between the plates, such as occur when driving through bends are equalized by the VC, which in this way performs the function of a central differential and prevents wind-up in the drive train. With larger differences in rotational speed, such as when a wheel suddenly loses traction on ice, the connection between the two sets of plates becomes firmer and according to the degree of slippage a greater or lesser part of the total drive torque is diverted from the front to the rear wheels.

Normally, in dry conditions, the front axle of the Golf Syncro transmits most of the drive power, but when more traction is required, such as when accelerating, more power is transferred through the rear wheels, the amount of power transfer being regulated by the VC in fractions of a second. If, for example, the front wheels start to spin in extreme

conditions, almost all of the power is transferred through the rear wheels in order to achieve maximum propulsion and stability and, as far as possible, neutral driving characteristics. A freewheel is integrated into the rear differential, which automatically interrupts the power flow to the rear axle when braking and ensures complete compatibility of the 4WD system with the electronically controlled ABS. However, the freewheel is bypassed in reverse gear by an electro-pneumatically actuated dog clutch in order that permanent 4WD is still available and more torque is transmitted to the axle for the wheels offering the most grip.

The Golf Syncro entered production five months after it had been seen in prototype form at the 1985 Frankfurt show. The permanent 4WD system was initially confined to five-door cars carrying a CL level of exterior and interior equipment and powered by 90bhp carburettor-equipped or, for some markets, fuel-injected and catalyst-equipped 1,781cc engines of the same power output. However, there was little doubt that in due course the transmission would be extended

Having produced a Golf with permanent four-wheel drive it was only logical to develop the theme a stage further by introducing a high-ground-clearance derivative for off-road work. This is a 1991 version of the Golf Country with reinforced front protection bars.

Two years earlier the off-road Golf had appeared as a design study, when it had carried the provisional name Montana. The 1.8-litre fuel-injected engine was the chosen power unit.

to the Golf GTI and some of its high-performance derivatives. In the meantime, the Golf Syncro in its initial guise was given something of a sporting flavour externally with a large front spoiler, flared wheelarches, black sill trims and wide body side protection strips, and internally by a four-spoke sports steering wheel as well as the luxury touch of a padded dashboard and a centre console.

A second model, the similarly powered Golf GT Syncro, was introduced in 1987 to offer a higher level of both interior and exterior trim and, most importantly, standard ABS braking. The intention here was to reinforce Volkswagen's claim that the Syncro system offered a combination of permanent 4WD, slip-dependent power distribution through a viscous coupling, and unrestricted ABS compatibility through a freewheel, something which again no other manufacturer was providing in this category of car.

Although the Golf Syncro weighed between 90 and 100kg more than an equivalent front-drive model, performance figures were found not to be significantly affected, and Volkswagen claimed a 0–62mph (100km/h) figure of 11.3sec and a top speed of 111mph (178km/h), with equivalent figures of 12sec and 109mph (175km/h) for the catalyst version.

The layout of the 4WD system required changes in the running gear as compared with the front-drive Golfs, and at the rear a semi-trailing arm axle was provided in conjunction with MacPherson suspension struts and stiffer springs and dampers, plus a separate anti-rollbar. Uprated springs and dampers were also fitted at the front, and the diameter and width of the rear drum brakes was increased. The floorpan had to be redesigned at the rear, and the 55-litre/12.1-gallon fuel tank had to be reshaped to the available space. Even so, a

The revisions at the rear of the Golf necessary to incorporate the Syncro drive to the rear wheels included the adoption of semi-trailing-arm suspension. In this display chassis the viscous coupling has been cut away to reveal the multiple steel plates which help to control the drive.

penalty of the Syncro system was that luggage space was reduced to 230 litres (VDA), but this was compensated for (on both the CL and the GT Syncro) by providing a split rear folding seat and backrest giving up to 1,030 litres of space when the car was reduced to a two-seater.

Rallye Golf

The Rallye Golf, the most exciting derivative of the Mark 2 model produced thus far, had barely been announced in 1989 when it became a victim of its potential success. The sport's governing body ruled that its supercharged engine had to carry a 40mm restrictor in its intake system, thereby effectively

limiting its power output to around 230bhp at a time when cars with turbocharged engines could develop close to 300bhp. Although, following an appeal, this restriction was deferred for one season, it effectively killed the long-term competition career of an impressive new car. Nevertheless, the Rallye Golf was not merely a competition car; its advanced specification also ensured it a special place in the affections of high-performance enthusiasts as a road car of particular merit.

Sitting on 15in multi-spoke alloy wheels shod with low-profile tyres and nestling beneath flared wheelarches, the 5,000 cars, all of them assembled with left-hand drive at a VW factory in Belgium, combined a 160bhp G-lader engine

featuring charge air cooling and regulated emissions control (by lambda probe and catalytic converter) with the syncro 4WD system, electronically controlled ABS braking and power steering, as well as providing a high level of standard or optional equipment.

In Volkswagen's G-lader system, the supercharger, which is driven from the engine via a ribbed belt, comprises a housing, a displacer with scroll-shaped vanes, the driveshaft with eccentric and the displacer guide. The displacer with its scrolls moves eccentrically in a G-shaped housing, shifting the air drawn in through chambers; even at high revs, only low relative speeds occur between the housing and the displacer, thereby increasing service life.

The air, which is heated up through the displacement in the supercharger, is then cooled and made more dense by being passed through a charge air cooler on its way into the engine, which also helps to reduce knock sensitivity. On part load, more air is delivered to the engine than it can absorb, so the surplus is returned to the intake duct of the charger via a bypass valve controlled mechanically by the throttle valve.

At the time of the G-lader's launch, Volkswagen expressed

Uniquely amongst European Mark 2 Golfs, the Rallye has its dual head-lamps recessed behind rectangular lenses. This limited-production car was only made in left-hand-drive form, but nevertheless it is highly coveted in the UK.

The flared body panels give the G60-engined Rallye an aggressively distinct appearance, which is reinforced by the use of 15in multi-spoke wheels with low-profile tyres.

the view that the G-shaped supercharger had remained unused for so long (the principle dates back to a French patent taken out in 1905) because prior to the introduction of automation for the production of light metal castings, no manufacturer had been able to handle the casting and milling processes with sufficient precision to produce the two housing shells in aluminium and the displacer in magnesium with the required accuracy in large quantities.

The Rallye Golf's engine differed from the other 1.8-litre units in that its cylinder dimensions of 80.6mm bore and 86.4mm stroke gave a displacement of 1,763cc instead of the familiar 1,781cc, this small reduction enabling the engine to fit more comfortably within the 2½-litre motorsport class limit after its true capacity had been multiplied by the factor of 1.4 applicable to supercharged engines. Operating with a compression ratio of 8:1 and a maximum supercharger boost pressure of 0.65bar, the engine gave a power output of 160bhp at 5,600rpm in standard tune. Maximum torque was an impressive 163lb/ft (225Nm) at 4,000rpm, with 145lb/ft (200Nm) or more available from 2,400 to 5,600rpm. Mixture preparation was by the Digifant electronic injection system incorporating digital control and regulation of the ignition, and injection was via engine maps and incorporated an overrun cut-out, idle speed stabilization and selective knock sensing.

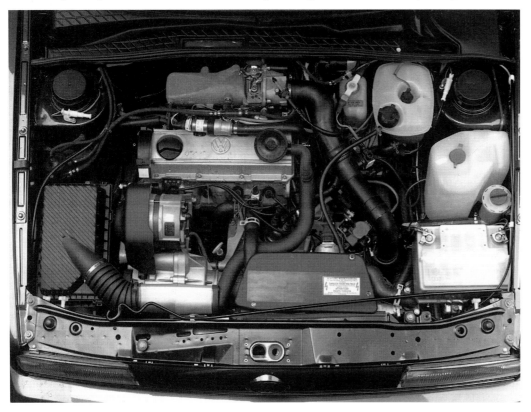

The under-bonnet layout of one of the most exciting of all Golfs, the 160bhp G60-powered Rallye. The installation includes charge air cooling as well as a lambda probe and catalytic converter to control emissions.

The cockpit of a standard production version of the Rallye, a car which had been conceived for competitions and might well have had a long and brilliant career had it not encountered an untimely change in regulations.

Transmission of the Rallye Golf's considerable power into the Syncro system was entrusted to the new type O2A five-speed manual gearbox which had already been proven in the latest Passat and the recently announced Corrado coupe. A precise and light shift action had been obtained by combining a bearing-mounted selector shaft and cable operation, while tapered roller bearings directly on the drive pinion helped to promote quiet running, the soft mounting and cable operation meaning that less drive train noise was transmitted to the passenger compartment.

The Rallye Golf was equipped with 205/50VR-15 tyres mounted on 6J x 15in alloy wheels and the car was set 20mm lower than the Golf Syncro. The springs and sports shock absorbers, with higher damping rates than on the Golf GTI 16V, were specially matched and stronger anti-rollbars were fitted.

When they announced the car, Volkswagen claimed a 0–50mph acceleration time of 5.6sec and to 62mph (100km/h) in 8.6sec, with a top speed of 130mph. Equipment unique to the model included front and rear bumpers with integrated aprons, a special radiator grille and broad-beam headlamps and foglamps located in the bumper; front and rear spoilers, green-tinted glass, an electronically amplified roof aerial for the stereo equipment and remote-control exterior mirrors were also part of the specification. The spoilers, bumpers, apron, radiator and mirrors were all finished in the car's body colour.

The two front sports seats were height-adjustable and part-leather trimmed, leather also being used for the rim of the four-spoke steering wheel, the front head restraints and the side panel trim. The rear seat back was split-folding. Amongst the optional extras for the Rallye Golf were a sunroof, electrically heated and controlled exterior mirrors, electric window lifts, central locking, Recaro sports seats, rear head restraints and various radio/cassette players with multiple speakers. However, a special equipment package, comprising the sunroof, central locking, electric windows and electrically operated and heated remote-control door mirrors, was offered in the UK for an additional £1,045 over the normal cost of the Rallye.

Golf GTI G60

In February 1990, as total Golf GTI production approached the 900,000 mark, a new flagship model, the G60, was introduced to sit above the eight-valve and 16V in the product range. As already indicated, in broad terms the G60 was a logical series-production development of the Rallye Golf and it was the fourth VW to feature the potent cocktail of the eight-valve engine with the G-lader, the forced-

induction system which had also been brought to market aboard the new Corrado G60 coupe and the Passat GT Syncro. Unlike the Rallye Golf, which was confined to the three-door bodyshell, the G60 was offered with the choice of three-door or five-door bodywork

The model lacked the flared wheelarches which were the most distinctive feature of the Rallye Golf, but in addition to its badging on the radiator grille and rear panel, the 160bhp (118kW) G60 could be recognized by a keen Golf observer by its 15in wheels and possibly by its further lowered running gear (2cm/0.8in at the front and 1cm/0.4in at the rear compared with the eight-valve GTI, whereas the regular 16V was just 1cm/0.4in lower at each end). Damper settings were modified to retain an acceptable level of ride comfort and Teflon-coated low-friction suspension struts similar to those

The Golf GTI G60, a car built on the back of the technology developed for the Rallye, and in this instance available with both three-door and five-door bodywork.

A G60 in three-door trim, featuring the attractive BBS small-spoke alloy wheels. The flared wing panels of the Rallye were not adopted for the later car, which also retained the regular GTI four-headlamp grille.

The innocent looking rear end of a five-door G60, with little apart from the small model badge to indicate that its performance is anything out of the ordinary.

used on the Passat were introduced. Front and rear spring characteristics matched those for the 16V model, but the front anti-rollbar diameter was increased from the 18mm of the two lower-powered GTIs to 23mm, while the rear bar diameter went up slightly from the 20mm of the other cars to 21mm.

ABS braking became part of the G60's standard equipment and VW's electronic differential lock (EDL), which makes use of some of the ABS componentry, was offered as an option. Power-assisted steering and 185/55VR-15 tyres on 6in wheel rims were also standardized, although 195/50VR-15 tyres on 6½in-rimmed BBS wheels were available as a factory-fitted extra-cost option. The BBS wheels also formed part of an Edition One extra-equipment package which in addition included Recaro sports seats, a leather-covered steering wheel and gearshift gaiter, chrome-treated rear side and tailgate windows, partially darkened rear light clusters and white front turn signal lenses. The G60 Edition One was also offered exclusively in a range of metallic exterior finishes.

There is quite a tight fit beneath the bonnet of the GTI G60 with the addition of the supercharger – seen low down in the foreground – and the plumbing of the charge air cooling arrangements to be accommodated.

At a time when so many other manufacturers favoured turbocharging as a means for boosting power output, Volkswagen's adoption of the G-lader was a bold move, but the company explained that the advantages of a mechanically driven supercharger over a turbocharger, the turbine performance of which is influenced by exhaust gas flow, were fundamental to its aim of achieving greater engine power with high levels of low-speed torque and minimal throttle lag. When announcing the G60, the company claimed that 80% of full charge pressure was available through the G-lader within 0.4sec of opening the throttle and full pressure within a further 0.4sec. The high-torque characteristics were confirmed by the evidence of figures showing that in excess of 145lb/ft (200Nm) was available from 2,400rpm to 5,800rpm

– the crankshaft speed at which peak power was seen – with a maximum torque of 163lb/ft (225Nm) being seen at 3,800rpm.

By coupling the engine to the company's new MQ gearbox, offering a set of relatively low and closely spaced ratios, the claimed top speed of 134mph (216km/h) was achieved in fifth gear at 5,680rpm, while in the same gear the car would accelerate from 50 to 75mph (80 to 120km/h) in 11sec, compared with 12.9sec with the 16V and 13.1sec with the standard GTI. Acceleration from standstill to 62mph (100km/h) occupied 8.3sec in the G60 compared with 9.0sec in the 16V and 10.3sec in the eight-valve GTI. Understandably, the G60 has become a most highly coveted member of the Golf GTI family.

The lower ride height of the GTI G60 can be seen clearly in this view of a 1990 model, with the 15-inch BBS wheels and 195/50-section tyres nestling closely beneath the wheel-arch extensions. The discreet 'GTI' badge let into the side rubbing strip is typical of the understated nature of this car.

Where it all happens. The spoke layout of the G60's steering wheel leaves a clear view of the main instrument dials, which are separated by the temperature gauge, the panel of 10 warning lights and the computer readout.

The upholstery and door trim of a 1990 three-door GTI G60 was similar to that of other high-performance models in the Golf range. Note the generous depth of the seat cushions.

The internals of the 1.8-litre G60 engine with its belt-driven forced induction system exposed. The engine was developed from the eight-valve version of the EA 827 unit.

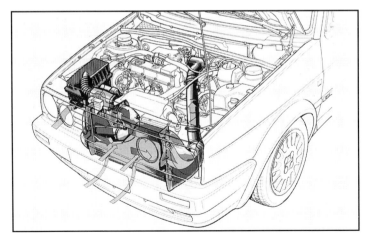

A drawing showing how the side-mounted charge air cooler for the G60 was integrated into the Golf's regular engine cooling system.

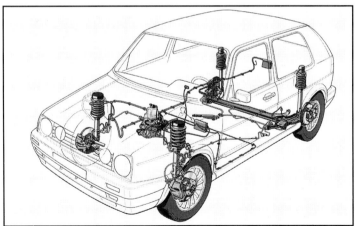

The development of an electronic anti-lock braking system for the highest-performing Golfs involved some complicated pipework.

CHAPTER 9

Jetta Mark 2

No longer an afterthought

Developed this time as an integral part of the Mark 2 range, the Jetta, launched in January 1984, was conceived as a two-door or four-door saloon in its own right (of which the four-door would prove by far the more popular) rather than as another Golf with a boot. It did, though, share much of the Golf's mechanical specification and was offered initially with a choice of all three sizes of carburettor-fed engine which were available for the Golf (1.3, 1.6 and 1.8-litre) as well as a pair of 1.6-litre diesels, one of them turbocharged.

The grafting of a huge 23cu ft boot on to the back of the car increased its overall length from the 398.5cm of the Golf to 431.5cm; in other words, the Jetta required an extra 13in in the parking bay. The Golf and Jetta, of course, shared the same 247.5cm wheelbase, both models thereby benefiting from a considerable improvement in rear-seat legroom compared with the equivalent Mark 1 version. Although the deep boot gave the Jetta a somewhat heavy appearance, its aerodynamic Cd of 0.36 (compared with the Golf's 0.34) was a pleasant surprise from a 'three-box' car of this bulk. In some markets, the Jetta was supplied with a space-saver spare wheel, but a full-size spare was standard equipment for the UK market, an uneven load floor being the penalty. Also, somewhat surprisingly, there was no fold-down rear seat facility to extend the luggage space further.

Although the Golf and Jetta had much in common from the doors forward, the new saloon was instantly recognizable by a smoother grille which was flanked by rectangular rather than circular headlamps. Four levels of equipment were offered, identified with the model designations C, CL, GL

and GLX, the latter being the equivalent in some markets, including the USA, of the Carat. Although the base model, the C was scarcely spartan and included useful items like reclining seats, head restraints, halogen headlamps, reversing lights, intermittent wipers, a parcels shelf and cloth seat and door trim. The CL provided in addition a centre console, radio, clock, trip meter, extra air vents and door bins, while the GL added such items as remote-control door mirrors, additional side mouldings, a rev-counter and a door-operated courtesy light with delay switch. At the top of the range, the GLX or Carat offered metallic paint, power-steering, electric window lifts all round, central locking, electrically adjustable and heated door mirrors, velour upholstery, a stereo radio/cassette player, a multi-function dashboard computer, rear head restraints and a rear centre armrest which, when lowered, exposed a small access hole for carrying skis or similarly long and thin objects.

Like the equivalent Golf models, 1.3-litre Jettas were supplied with a four-speed manual transmission, but the larger-engined cars were available with either a conventional or a 4+E five-speed manual transmission and were also offered in three-speed automatic-transmission form. On 1.6-litre cars 175/70SR-13 tyres on 5½J wheels were standard equipment with 185/60SR-14 on 5½J or 6J alloy wheels optional.

The performance profile of the Jetta was raised considerably in October 1984 with the announcement of a Jetta GT powered by the 112bhp 1.8-litre engine of the Golf GTI, or a version with catalytic converter and lambda sensor

The extra spaciousness offered with the Mark 2 version of the Jetta was emphasized by the high roof line of the luggage compartment. This is an early GLX, the top model of the line when it was introduced into the UK market.

The front and rear compartments of the Jetta GLX, on which central locking, electric windows and heated and electrically adjustable door mirrors were all part of the standard specification.

The well-equipped interior of the Jetta GLX, which included high-quality upholstery and door trim. A blanking plate still covers the space normally occupied by the car's radio

The simpler steering wheel, different upholstery and manual winders for the windows identify this as a Jetta GL.

mixture control developing 107bhp for the USA and other emissions-conscious markets. Identified by an extended front apron and a discreet spoiler on the bootlid, and usually seen wearing a set of multiple-slot alloy wheels, it was a great success. Its combination of refinement, performance and practicality, including a 0–60mph acceleration time of 9sec and a top speed of 117mph in 112bhp form (and only fractionally slower with a catalyst), proved an attractive proposition to many customers who previously had considered the Jetta to be a trifle stodgy, not least because whatever the engine between the front wheels it had to haul something like 30kg more weight than in an equivalent Golf. The GT came with disc brakes all round, ventilated at the front, a load-sensitive brake pressure regulator and a brake booster servo, a rear anti-rollbar and the five-speed manual gearbox. Inside, the Jetta GT was supplied with sports front seats, a four-spoke steering wheel, a leather-covered gearshift knob, full instrumentation and the seven-function computer display. For 1987, a stereo radio/cassette player became standard equipment on Jettas along with a height-adjustable driver's seat (the striped cloth trim of which was matched on the door panels), a trip computer, central locking, polished steel wheels and heater vents for the rear passengers.

The most important Jetta development in 1987 was the introduction of the 16V version to sit above the eight-valve GT, which on the UK market was simultaneously rebadged as a GTi. The 16-valve engine has already been described in some detail in the context of its application to the Golf, and it suffices here to mention that its specification in the Jetta was identical apart from a longer exhaust system to match the saloon's extended bodywork. Like the equivalent Golf, the Jetta 16V's ride height was lowered by 10mm compared with the eight-valve GTi, which meant that it sat 2cm lower than carburettor-engined Jettas and looked much the better for this. The 185/60 tyres of the 16V were VR rather than HR-rated and they were fitted to different-style 6J x 14in wheels which could also be found on the recently introduced Golf Clipper Convertible. With nearly 140bhp on tap, the 16-valve Jetta was a car with a performance which belied its still discreet appearance, and when put to the test it could raise more than a few eyebrows.

In 1988, when the Golf underwent a series of cosmetic changes, the Jetta was given similar treatment, including a

Introduced to the UK market in 1986, the Jetta GT was fitted with the same 1.8-litre fuel-injected engine as the Golf GTI. The car also had lowered and stiffened suspension, disc brakes all round, front and rear spoilers and wheelarch extensions.

The 16-valve engine found its way into the Jetta during the 1987 season, although volume sales did not begin until 1988. When the car was previewed the '16V' appendage was placed beneath a 'GT' badge, but later cars were produced carrying the more familiar 'GTI' designation on the grille.

Body changes during 1988 ran parallel to those made to the Golf and included a new and bolder grille, full-width door windows with repositioned mirrors and wider mouldings along the body sides.

The TX, introduced into the UK market in 1985, was to become the best-selling Jetta model from 1986 to 1990. Its combination of the 1.6-litre carburettor engine and a number of GTi-type features such as 14in wheels, wheelarch extensions and body spoilers gave it a popularity mirroring that of the Driver within the Golf range.

bold new grille – incorporating in this instance just three horizontal bars – and subtle changes to the bumpers and body side mouldings. A small but important change was the repositioning of the rear-view mirrors further forward on the front doors and the deletion of the quarterlights. Detail specifications were raised on the lower-priced models, the base model receiving the additional air vents on the facia and the wider body rubbing strips and the CL larger trays in the doors, but in the UK electric window lifts and power-steering joined a growing list of options at the top of the range, which included metallic paint, air conditioning and leather trim. A realignment of model designations at this point meant that the range started with the Jetta (the C suffix had been dropped), followed by the CL (also available since 1986 as a Syncro), GL, GTX and GTX 16V, the last two being the cars with fuel-injected engines.

However, in 1989 the Jetta range was simplified from five to three models, the base model being deleted and the GT and GTX being combined into one version carrying the GT badge, the other designations being CL and GL. There were

A 1990 Jetta GTi 16V with the latest deep front and rear bumpers and aprons, its high-performance potential underlined by the BBS alloy wheels and low-profile tyres. The rear-mounted roof aerial was a familiar feature on 16V-engined cars.

The internal workings of the 16-valve engine revealed. The small 25deg angle between the two sets of valves enabled the light-alloy cylinder head to be kept conveniently narrow.

a number of changes to the standard equipment of all three models, which included for the CL a higher grade of upholstery for the seats, doors and side panel trim. The GL was only to be available in future with four-door bodywork and with the 1.6-litre the smallest engine. A four-spoke steering wheel, power-assisted steering, central locking and high-quality velour upholstery and carpeting became part of the standard specification, but the previously fitted electrically adjustable door mirrors were replaced with mirrors having interior manual remote control. The GT model, which absorbed the former GTD and GTX versions, was only available as a four-door car and now had new velour trim, sports seats with height adjustment on the driver's side and 185/60HR-14 tyres on 6J x 14in steel wheels.

For the CL, the range of engines started with the 1,272cc 55bhp (40kW), followed by the 1,595cc 72bhp (53kW) and the 1,781cc 84bhp (62kW), all with carburettors and unregulated catalysts meeting European standards. For the US market there was the 1,595cc 79bhp (51kW), with electronically regulated carburettor, and the 1,272cc 55bhp

A Syncro version of the Jetta CL was offered from 1988, although very few cars found their way on to the UK market. This is a German-registered 1990 model.

(40kW) and 1,781cc 90bhp (66kW), both with fuel injection, all three engines having catalyst and lambda probe. The 1,588cc 54bhp (40kW) diesel and 70bhp (51kW) turbodiesel, which were only available with manual transmission, also met USA requirements. Other than the 1,272cc carburettor version, all the engines were also available with the Jetta GL. The GT was offered with the 1,781cc carburettor engine producing 84bhp (62kW) in European specification, or either the 90bhp (66kW) Mono-Jetronic or the 107bhp (79kW) Digifant injection versions with lambda regulation. Finally, the GT 16V delivered 129bhp (95kW), a catalyst and lambda probe to US requirements now being this engine's standard specification. Only available with four-door bodywork, the GT 16V, which could still be identified by the red grille badge and the electrically powered aerial at the rear of the roof, continued to be fitted with stiffer springs, dampers and anti-rollbars and had larger pistons for the ventilated front and solid rear disc brakes.

The 4WD Jetta Syncro, for which the standard engine was the 1,781cc 90bhp (66kW) with Digifant fuel injection, was available to either CL or GT specification, which matched that of the front-drive models but with the addition of ABS braking, a folding rear seat, lateral turn signals, a rev-counter and a digital clock.

From 1990, all Jettas had redesigned bumpers, and black wheelarch and body sill extensions became standard across the range along with a remote-control nearside mirror and 6J x 14in steel wheels. Diesel versions had their engines uprated and 'cleaned' by charge air cooling, which previously had been available only on Passat models. For the turbodiesel this meant a 10bhp increase to 80bhp (59kW). By now, the Jetta had almost run its course, for a Mark 3 version of the Golf was imminent, which meant that Mark 2 production would be run down, at least in Germany. Over a production life of more than seven years, though, the Jetta had enhanced its reputation as much more than a 'three-box' Golf; it had sought and had justly earned recognition as a car of considerable merit in its own right.

A parade of 1990-specification Jettas, with the two-door version in the foreground, a reasonably commonplace model in Germany but comparatively rare in the UK.

One of the last models in the Mark 2 Jetta family, this GX was the best seller of the reduced range in 1991, its combination of upmarket sporting appendages and a competitive price proving a considerable attraction.

CHAPTER 10

Golf range in the Rabbit warren

Golfs and derivatives in the United States

Since the United States had provided the foundation for the Beetle's international success and become by far its most important and lucrative export market, it was understandable that Volkswagen should wish to do everything possible to build and sustain equal Stateside enthusiasm for its successor.

In a sense the Beetle had been a unique phenomenon because it had been an inherited and essentially out-of-date design which no other manufacturer had sought to challenge by offering a similar concept. The situation in the United States with the Golf, however, was certain to be very different. Although it represented something of a new direction in small car design (the qualification here is justified because it was by no means the first 'two-box' design – remember Pininfarina's Austin A40, for example?) it was a car which, if it proved as successful as Volkswagen required it to be, other manufacturers would not be slow in copying. Furthermore, any challenge of this sort was at least as likely to emanate from Japan as from Europe, and if it did so it was more than likely to be backed up by some vigorously competitive pricing and marketing.

This was part of the thinking behind Volkswagen's longer-term strategic plan to establish a local assembly plant in the United States from where the bulk of the market's requirements could be supplied. Apart from eliminating the transatlantic shipping costs, the establishment of a separate VW factory geared to the needs of the North American market would also enable changes of specification to be made to suit local requirements more readily than on the production lines at Wolfsburg.

However, before such a bold venture could be sanctioned it was essential to establish that the new car had indeed captured American hearts in a similar way to the Beetle and that the market could sustain output from a local factory at an economic level. It was not until 1978 that VW of America's plant at Westmoreland County, Pennsylvania, finally came on stream, prior to which all US-specification cars continued to be supplied from Germany.

The first item of the Golf's specification to be changed for the American market was its name, and what better name than Rabbit to suggest that the car was quick off the mark, had a fine turn of speed, could change direction with remarkable agility, was compact, good looking and a whole lot of fun?

As in Europe, the first models to be offered were the mainstream three-door and five-door sedans (saloons) with the 1,471cc engine, which with Bosch K-Jetronic fuel injection – in order to meet the required emissions standards – delivered 71bhp at 5,800rpm and torque of 73lb/ft at 3,500rpm. But as Rabbits tended to be 100 to 200lb heavier than the equivalent Golfs (depending upon the level of mandatory emissions and safety equipment at the time) the availability from 1976 of the larger-bore 1,588cc engine came as something of a relief. Equipped with similar Bosch injection, this engine boosted power output of the Rabbit to 90bhp at 5,500rpm and torque to approximately 85lb/ft at 3,300rpm. However, by 1979 the engine had given way to a shorter-stroke (73.4mm) derivative with a displacement of just 1,457cc. With this, the power and torque figures were

The Rabbits emerging from VW's Pennsylvania factory were visibly different from their German Golf counterparts, notably at the front, where a different grille incorporated rectangular light units. The mandatory bumpers did little to enhance the appearance of this 1981 Rabbit S.

reduced to 72bhp at 5,800rpm and 72lb/ft at 3,500rpm, respectively, and power output was further strangled later to a modest 63bhp at 5,400rpm, although simultaneously torque was improved slightly to 75lb/ft at 3,500rpm.

The Rabbit was not really let off the leash until the introduction of the 1,716cc engine when the Westmoreland factory began to supply cars. The displacement was the result of combining the familiar 79.5mm bore with the longer stroke of 86.4mm, and with the usual Bosch equipment installed power and torque figures were restored to the more respectable levels of 75bhp at 5,000rpm and 88lb/ft at 3,000rpm.

In general, the Rabbit range had been well received, but it had not been all plain sailing for the Volkswagen management because during the early days of the new car the company had had to contend with a rash of complaints about sub-standard detail quality and poor reliability. This had been deeply disappointing to people used to the quality and dependability of the Beetle, and it would have been severely damaging to VW's image but for the widespread awareness of and admiration for the Rabbit's inherent qualities. Clearly, the car was a potential winner, and as Volkswagen acted swiftly to put right the deficiencies which had been identified, and leant heavily on any dealer who seemed reluctant to respond in an acceptable way to what was clearly only a temporary problem, customer loyalty was restored.

Later, when Westmoreland-built cars began to pour on to the market, there was a further bout of criticism concerning some of the subtle changes in detail specification which had been aimed at 'softening up' the cars for the US market. Nor was there any widespread welcome for some of the more garish attempts to jazz-up both the external styling and the interior trim and decor of cars which, because of the emissions restrictions imposed on their small engines, could scarcely be called pocket rockets. When sales of these cars fell well below expectations there was a rapid rethink of policy and before long cars were coming down the line which offered the taut handling and understated appearance which was synonymous with the products of Wolfsburg.

News of the popularity of the GTI throughout Europe had spread quickly to North America, but it was not until 1978 that the car began to cross the Atlantic, and then only into the Canadian market. The cars imported there were virtually identical to their European equivalents apart from a pair of US-specification impact-resistant bumpers and the use of steel wheels with the narrower 5in rims as used on the regular Golf, shod in this instance with 175/70SR-13 tyres. However, alloy wheels were available as an optional extra on Canada-bound GTIs.

The desire for a high-performance model in the United States would not be properly satisfied until the first Rabbit GTI left the Westmoreland factory in 1982, but in the meantime an interim Rabbit S was offered which combined the European GTI's suspension and interior package, including the sports seats, with the American-market 1,716cc engine in its normal state of tune.

The launch of the Rabbit GTI had been held back pending the successful completion of the development of a US-specification version of the 1,781cc engine which was earmarked for the European GTI from 1982. This operated with a compression ratio of 9.5:1, compared with the 10:1 compression of the European engine; it retained the camshaft from the 1,716cc US engine for more low-speed flexibility and it provided maximum power of 91bhp at 5,500rpm and

A US-market 1978 Scirocco with high-back front seats. In this instance the substantial bumpers had a more integrated appearance.

A 1980 Scirocco S with deep front airdam and decorative stripes along the body sides and on the C-pillar. By this time the seats had been given separate adjustable head restraints.

Not all Rabbits are what they seem to be. This badge, in fact, was spotted on the back of a right-hand-drive 1983 UK-registered Golf GTI.

98lb/ft of torque at 3,000rpm. The same ratios were adopted for the five-speed gearbox, but the American cars had a 3.94:1 final-drive ratio in place of the 3.65:1 then being supplied with European-built GTIs.

The extra weight of the US emissions equipment, the mandatory '5mph' bumpers and the air conditioning which was so vital in much of the market – notably California and the southern states – meant that the Rabbit GTI required very different springing from that of the Golf GTI. Consequently the Rabbit's spring rates ended up 22% stiffer at the front and 29% at the rear and its dampers were also uprated. Another change from the European GTI specification concerned the wheels, the Golf's 5½J x 13in alloys being discarded in favour of the 6J x 14in alloys from the latest Passat, or Quantum as it was known in the USA. The wheels were fitted with lower-profile 185/60HR-14 Pirelli P6 tyres.

Apart from the impact-resisting bumpers and the different wheels and tyres, the principal external difference between this car and its European counterpart was the pair of rectangular headlamps inboard of substantial separate parking lamps and flanking a slightly different grille. Inside the car the main changes from Golf GTI specification were the corduroy finish to the special sports-type front seats and the brushed aluminium facing of the main instrument nacelle and the three-dial sub-assembly on the centre console.

Having sampled some of the less acceptable products from Westmoreland, serious car-testers were fearing the worst from the Rabbit GTI, but instead were enthralled by it, echoing in nearly every respect the enthusiasm shown earlier for the European-built car. It was the combination of

The rebodied US Scirocco was fitted with a longer-stroke 1.7-litre version of the 1.6-litre engine used on European cars. Rubber strips were used to protect the body sides and bright trim strips relieved the heaviness of the bumpers. This 1982 car carries a 'Fuel Injection' plate on the tailgate, but unlike European cars, there is no model designation on the B-pillar.

The Rabbit name was dropped when the Mark 2 hatchback was introduced into the US market, the regular cars adopting the Golf name, but the high-performance model being known simply as the VW GTI. Note the mandatory repeater lights on the front wings.

performance with refinement which so impressed, and just as the GTI had helped to increase the flow of buyers into the showrooms of Europe in search of other Golf models, so were Rabbits of all breeds suddenly in more demand again once the news of the GTI's exceptional qualities had been spread around, even though the car was already six years old when it entered the US market and its basic design a year older still and destined to be replaced two years hence.

Although the Rabbit was the principal contender in VW's US market (the convertible joining the hatchbacks from 1980), the Scirocco had also been available since 1975, usually with the same power options. This meant that it entered the market with the 1,471cc engine, was then upgraded to the 1,588cc unit for the 1978 model year and elevated again to 1,716cc in 1981. This was the engine which accompanied the rebodied car on its introduction in time for the 1982 season. Then in 1983 the Scirocco became available with the 1,781cc engine which, even with full emissions gear installed, put out a more useful 90bhp.

Meanwhile, the Jetta had joined the Rabbit in the United States in 1980 as a 1,588cc car and, like the hatchback, received the more torquey 1,716cc engine in 1981. Then, in 1984, several months after the introduction of the rebodied hatchbacks came the Mark 2 version of the Jetta with both the carburettor-equipped and the fuel-injected 1,781cc engines.

The lessons of the Mark 1 had not been forgotten and from the beginning the Mark 2 cars which left the Westmoreland production lines were very much closer to the European specification except, of course, in respect of the mandatory emissions and safety equipment. This time, the Rabbit name was buried and Golf was adopted instead, although not for the high-performance hatch, which was to be known simply as the Volkswagen GTI; this car has only been available with three-door bodywork on the US market.

As with the Mark 1, the Mark 2 product range in the United States has been built around the Golf hatchback and convertible, the Jetta and the Scirocco, with the 1,716cc and 1,781cc engines predominating. The 16-valve version of the latter was added to the range, replacing the eight-valve version in the GTI, for the 1987 season. With full three-way catalytic equipment and less radical valve timing aimed at enhancing low-speed torque, this engine offered 123bhp at 5,800rpm and 120lb/ft of torque at 4,250rpm, compared with 105bhp at 5,400rpm and 107lb/ft at 3,400rpm for the Digifant-injected eight-valve engine still used in Golf and Jetta GL models.

A further significant engine change occurred in 1990 when the 16-valve top end was grafted on to the block of the 1,984cc Passat engine to give the US-market Golf GTI and Jetta GLi a much more interesting power output of 134bhp at 5,800rpm and a healthy torque figure of 133lb/ft at 4,400rpm. Meanwhile, a further uprating of the eight-valve engine had resulted in an improvement in output to 105bhp at 5,400rpm and 110lb/ft at 3,400rpm.

As happened in Europe, the availability of more powerful engines for the Jetta from the mid-Eighties, accompanied by the policy of upgrading the specification of the top models (called the Carat in the USA and Germany, the GTX in the UK) with a lavish level of standard equipment, transformed the image of this four-door model from that of an efficient but unexciting family workhorse into an appealing alternative to the hatchback GTI.

Despite the constant stimulation of the US market with the help of annual limited-edition models, the encroachment of the Japanese into what had always been a highly competitive trading environment made it increasingly difficult for VW to justify the huge overhead of a local assembly plant at Westmoreland as the Eighties progressed. So with a dramatic downturn in the total car market during the second half of the decade the decision was taken to cease manufacture in Pennsylvania, after which all Mark 2 Golfs and their derivatives supplied to the US market were the products of VW's Mexican assembly plant. These have been difficult times for all car manufacturers, but the brand loyalty which Volkswagen has won through the Rabbit, Golf, Jetta and Scirocco runs deep and should ensure a healthy used-car market for these cars in the years to come.

CHAPTER 11

Corrado 16V, G60 and VR6

Volkswagen's Golf-derived sports coupe

Volkswagen's introduction of a Corrado coupe to sit above, rather than replace, the Scirocco was a case of third time lucky for a company which had long held aspirations of a slice of the sportscar market. The first attempt, a collaborative effort with Porsche, had led to the introduction at the end of 1969 of the 'ugly duckling' VW-Porsche 914, a car which found relatively few friends before it was quietly dropped from the catalogue three years later. Then, in November 1975, came another Porsche, the 924, which had begun life as a VW project but had been 'canned' by top management in 1973 during the nervous days following the Gulf oil crisis and handed over to Porsche for completion, assembly subsequently taking place at the Audi-NSU factory at Neckarsulm.

When news of the forthcoming Corrado leaked out in 1988, VW acted quickly to dispel fears that the Scirocco's demise was imminent. It was made clear that the new car, despite its solid top, had been conceived as a sportscar rather than a coupe and was intended as much as a challenger to other European and Japanese manufacturers of high-performance cars – including Porsche, whose 924, conveniently, was approaching the end of its production life – as it was meant to appeal to VW's existing customers who were eager to move further upmarket.

Although based on the floorpan of the Golf Mark 2, the Corrado was to have little if any visual identity with that or any other contemporary VW model. A three-door body was created in VW Design's own studio which offered smoothly flowing lines from a neat front panel incorporating fixed headlamps flanking a horizontal-bar grille, over a long bonnet and steeply raked windscreen to a roof panel terminating in a large rear hatch over a neatly rounded tail panel which offered minimal overhang behind the rear wheels. The bumpers and front and rear aprons were formed as units and constructed in impact-absorbing plastic-sheathed steel, the front spoiler having air inlets for brake, engine and, in the case of a supercharged version, charge air cooling.

Volkswagen's corrosion protection had always been above-average, but during the Eighties it had reached a new height, enabling the company to offer a three-year guarantee against paint defects and a six-year protection against through-rusting. On the Corrado, folded metal sections and joints on the doors, bonnet and tailgate were bonded and sealed and galvanizing was used in strategic areas, while phosphating, cataphoretic priming, cavity sealing, long-term underbody sealing and the fitment of plastic shields to the front wheelarches hinted at impressive longevity.

Two versions of the 1.8-litre Corrado were to be offered: the supercharged G60, the 160bhp performance of which could be translated into a top speed of around 140mph and, for the UK and Italian markets only, the 136bhp 16V, which was also no slouch with a top speed of over 130mph. The more slippery shape of the Corrado, therefore, had given it a slight edge over the equivalent Golf towards the top of the speed range, although its greater weight (by close to 400lb) somewhat blunted its acceleration up to 60mph, which in the G60 took approximately 9sec and the 16V almost a second longer.

Like both the eight-valve supercharged and 16-valve

The Corrado 16V, which was available in the UK in RHD form from the start, can be identified by its 16-spoke wheels. The spoiler on the tailgate adjusts automatically as the speed increases but can be raised through a control in the cockpit when required.

normally aspirated engines, the Corrado's front suspension, incorporating lower wishbones and MacPherson struts, was shared with the equivalent high-performance Golfs, but a key to the new car's outstanding handling and nimbleness was its rear suspension, a new development of the torsion-beam layout which had been used from the earliest Golfs and Sciroccos and which at the time of the Corrado's launch had already demonstrated its worth on the latest Passat range. Special bearings had been attached to the trailing arms from the cross-beam which would react to cornering forces and allow a subtle adjustment within predetermined limits of the rear track, thereby offering an element of passive rear-wheel steer to enhance grip and help to neutralize handling in severe cornering conditions. The successful application of this new system with the well-tried front suspension had given the new car outstanding balance and traction, although there was some criticism of its low-speed ride quality.

The Corrado's five-speed gearbox, which had been developed to handle torque up to 230Nm, was also from the latest Passat, and was used in conjunction with a 3.45:1 final drive. Both the G60 and the 16V Corrados were offered with power-steering, but there were variations in brakes, wheels and tyres. Teves ABS brakes were standard on the G60, with 28cm front discs, whereas the 16V had 25.6cm discs, and the

G60 came equipped with 195/50VR-15 tyres on 6½J x 15in BBS spoked wheels, whereas 185/55VR-15 tyres on VW's own 6J x 15in alloy wheels were standard equipment on the 16V, although the G60's wheels and tyres could be specified as an optional extra.

Most sportscars are two-seaters, but the Corrado offered practical 2+2 accommodation, even if the rear compartment – split into two separate seats by a fixed central armrest – was somewhat restricted and perhaps a touch claustrophobic compared with that of the Scirocco, mainly because of the significant reduction of glass area and the upsweep of the waistline towards the tail. Despite the short tail, a reasonable 10.5cu ft of luggage space was provided, and with the folding rear seat backrest split 60/40% there was considerable versatility in carrying capacity, enabling a maximum of 29.4cu ft of space for luggage with both parts of the rear seat lowered. A neat piece of packaging was the fitment of a first-aid kit in the rear of the armrest, while a pocket in the top of the rear seat backrest and accessible either from the cockpit or through the rear hatch was provided for a warning triangle. Despite the compact overall dimensions, the cockpit area gave a useful 141cm of elbow room across the front seats and 133cm across the rear part of the compartment, where 89cm of headroom was provided.

The comparatively high tail meant that the driver had only mediocre rear three-quarter vision. However, low-speed manoeuvring would have been even more difficult but for one of the Corrado's most useful features, a moving rear spoiler, which was automatically raised by 5cm when the car reached a certain speed (this varied from 45mph to 75mph according to the market), then lowered itself again as the speed fell below about 12mph. VW claimed that when in the raised position the airfoil reduced rear wheel lift by up to 64%. The driver was provided with an override control switch on the facia enabling the blade to be moved whenever necessary, such as when needing to give the car a thorough clean.

The Corrado's instrument panel, incorporating three large circular dials, and its control layout were assembled into an L-shaped housing neatly integrating the upper facia and centre console. The open top part of the four-spoke steering wheel gave an unobstructed view of the instruments, of which the one on the left housed the readout panel of the multi-function computer which was operated through a stalk on the steering column.

The well-finished interior could perhaps best be described as 'quiet', with full tufted velour carpeting of the passenger and luggage areas and an almost complete absence of highlights to relieve the matt plastic furnishings. Well-shaped cushions and backrests compensated for the relative shallowness of the height-adjustable front seats, which were supplied with a subdued tartan-pattern cloth trim on the main wearing surfaces, leather upholstery, as for some of the upmarket Golf models, being a costly optional extra.

Front and rear foglamps, electrically heated and adjusted mirrors, a four-speed heater, a digital computer and green-tinted glass were all part of the Corrado's standard equipment, but surprisingly on a car that was considerably more expensive than a fully equipped and similarly powered Golf, such items as a sunroof, electric window lifts and leather-covered steering wheel were all on the Corrado's options list at first, although the window lifts and the leather-covered wheel were added to the standard specification within a year, as were leather trimming for the handbrake, gearshift gaiter and gear knob. Central locking, a height-adjustable steering column, a stereo radio/cassette player

An L-shaped housing integrates the Corrado's main instrument panel with the centre console very neatly, with large air vents flanking the three dials. The Corrado G60 quickly outsold the 16V once it became available in RHD form. Both models had this seven-bar grille at the start.

with automatic speed-dependent volume control, four speakers and anti-theft coding, as well as adjustable seatbelt anchorages, were also standard equipment.

The first Corrado 16V appeared in UK showrooms in August 1989, 11 months after the car had been announced in Germany, and it was available with right-hand drive from the start, whereas only LHD G60s were to be built for some time to come. However, when the RHD version went on sale in April 1991 the supercharged car quickly established itself as

Five-spoke wheels identify the car on the far left as the 2.9-litre V6-engined Corrado VR6, but the bolder four-bar grille was also adopted for the other models for the 1992 season. The G60 continued to be supplied with these BBS multi-spoke wheels.

the more popular model, outselling the 16V by more than two to one. The key to its success was not so much its extra 24bhp, but the substantial improvement in torque from the 119lb/ft at 4,800rpm of the 16V to 165lb/ft at 4,000rpm. This, accompanied by a virtual absence of any throttle lag, made the car considerably more pleasant to drive in the low-to-medium speed range.

The 16V had been expected to become a more attractive proposition when it received the new 1,984cc engine from the Golf 3 for the 1992 model year. Equipped with K-Motronic fuel injection and, unlike the previous engine, a regulated catalytic converter, its 136bhp peak power remained the same, but torque improved significantly to 132lb/ft at 4,400rpm. Yet initially the larger engine proved something of a disappointment, partly because it was linked to far from ideal gear ratios, and also because it lacked the smoothness of the 1,781cc power unit which had served VW so well. A more powerful and more refined version of the 2-litre engine, however, was believed to be on the way.

The larger 16V engine was only one of several changes made to the Corrado at that time, the most visible being that both models received a bolder grille, bringing them into line with other high-performance VWs. ABS braking was now standard for both models, along with a 69-litre/15.4-gallon fuel tank in place of the previous 55-litre/12.1-gallon tank.

There was also improved stereo radio/cassette equipment with a pull-out security facility, a torch key for the central locking, and the intermittent windscreen wipe was provided with a time delay that could be adjusted between 1.5 and 22 seconds. The 16V was now equipped with 6J x 15in Estoril alloy wheels as standard and the car was upholstered in a new Domino cloth trim.

At the time of its introduction, the G60 version had been commended for providing a level of performance typical of a 2.6-litre engine from a power unit of only 1.8 litres. However, in 1992 VW went one better by offering a Corrado VR6 powered by a 2,861cc version of the two-valves-per-cylinder V6 normally aspirated engine which had previously been seen in 2,792cc form in a Golf 3. With a peak output of 190bhp at 5,800rpm and maximum torque of 181lb/ft at 4,200rpm, this new Corrado VR6 flagship was a 145mph car with an ability to accelerate from 0–60mph in 6.4sec. The problem of transmitting so much torque through a pair of driven front wheels had been tackled in a commendably simple way, a measure of traction control being achieved by automatically applying gentle braking to one of the wheels immediately it revolved significantly quicker than the other. When the Corrado VR6 went on sale in the UK in August 1992, it seemed to have all the elements of a classic high-performance sportscar.

CHAPTER 12

Buying a used Golf or derivative

Selection, ownership and preservation

Between 1990 and 1992 a significant part of the used car market in the UK underwent a fundamental change under the combined influences of a prolonged and deepening economic depression and a dramatic escalation in automotive-related crime. Consequently, cars which previously had seemed to be beyond financial reach were suddenly affordable, having been burdened with a marked reduction in their residual value. On the other hand, some of them – notably those with a GTi or similarly emotive label – became increasingly vulnerable not only to 'conventional' theft, but also to joy-riding, an activity all too often ending in write-off crashes or destruction by fire. As a result, insurance premiums on these models, especially for younger drivers living in traditionally high-risk areas, became in many instances exorbitant.

For these people, the solution has been to investigate more closely other models in the chosen product range, cars which retain most of the basic attributes of the preferred hatch, saloon or coupe, but avoid the crippling premiums associated with the hottest version's perceived 'theft factor'. Fortunately for potential owners of a Mark 1 or 2 Golf, Jetta or Scirocco there has been no shortage of desirable alternatives because, as the previous chapters will have indicated, all three have traditionally been multi-model ranges from which it should not be too difficult to select an affordable choice. The Corrado, of course, is rather different, although even here the lower-powered version may sometimes qualify for a less awesome insurance premium.

Meanwhile, by 1992 the marked drop in residual values of these 'hot' derivatives had tended to strengthen the market for them amongst the more mature buyers who discovered that a GTI could then be bought for about two-thirds of what it might have cost them a year previously. For these people, a heavier than planned-for insurance premium has in many instances been an acceptable add-on cost to pay for the unexpected opportunity to have some fun.

The cost of insurance should not be considered in isolation, however, but rather as one – admittedly significant – element of a car's total cost of ownership. In this context, the Volkswagen owner is probably on firmer ground than most because the cars covered in this book are united not just by a large degree of commonality of their technical specification; they also share a reputation for excellent build quality, durability and reliability. The cost of replacement parts, as with most manufacturers, varies between the burdensome and the surprisingly cheap, but the owner of a used and unabused VW should not expect to incur a heavier than normal bill for routine wear-and-tear items. It scarcely needs emphasizing, of course, that at a time when cars are available in such abundance it is more sensible than ever to select one which is accompanied by a full and up-to-date service record, preferably one which has or can be authenticated by an approved VW agent.

But even the best maintained cars will gradually deteriorate, and it is unlikely, for example, that the vast majority of Mark 1 Golfs, the youngest of which will have been on the road since 1984 and the oldest for nearly a decade longer, will have completely escaped the ravages of time. Nevertheless, a rust-free example is not the rarity it might be imagined; VWs tend to rust through neglect rather than fair wear and tear. It will be appropriate, therefore, in carrying out an inspection, to work through a carefully compiled check list, concentrating on a few areas of the bodywork which are sometimes overlooked, but can be quite expensive to repair or restore. In what follows, from time to time references will be made specifically to Golfs, but the remarks may be taken to apply equally to other VWs sharing the component or feature in question.

Compared with most cars of similar age, the Volkswagens featured in this book will have worn well because for the most part they were put together with care in the first place. Inevitably, deterioration is more likely to be apparent in a Mark 1 than a Mark 2, not just because of age, but because in designing the younger car VW's team had the benefit of years of experience of the Mark 1 in service and were able to identify one or two weaker areas and address them.

When inspecting the bodywork of a Mark 1 a useful place to begin is the rear, where the lower edge of the tailgate is a potential troublespot as a result of water collecting there, and the seal around the rear window is similarly prone to deterioration. Also, the lower-specification models lacked the advantage of the pneumatic lift mechanism, the tailgate instead being supported by a metal strap. When closing the lid, it was first necessary to raise the strap in order to release it, and if this was not done, the strap inevitably became bent, after which the tailgate probably never again fitted correctly.

As on so many cars, the bottom of the doors are potential rust spots on the earlier bodies and it is as well to examine closely the door glass and windscreen surround areas and the tops of the front wing panels forward of the doors. Another vulnerable area is the metal surround to the sunroof, so if one is fitted, slide the roof back, climb carefully on to the body sill and take a close look at the periphery of the roof opening. Elsewhere on the bodywork, the usual inspection of wheelarches and sills is to be recommended; even though the VWs were not normally prone to problems in these areas, accident damage might well have resulted in repaired or replacement parts not being given the factory standard of protection. From 1981, cars were fitted with plastic wheelarch liners, which proved a most effective rust deterrent, and subsequently many earlier cars were retrofitted with them. However, they can, of course, hide trouble underneath, so a 1980 or earlier car fitted with liners should be examined with considerable care in these areas.

The under-bonnet area should also be free of problems unless the car has habitually been parked beneath overhanging trees. Not only water, but also small leaves and twigs can work their way through the grille ahead of the windscreen and if they are not cleared away regularly they can block the channel and entry into the drain tubes through which water is supposed to be released under the car. If water is trapped in this area it can penetrate the wiper mechanism and even work its way into the bulkhead and leave the driver and front passenger with wet feet!

Turning to the mechanical inspection, any car from the Golf and associated families which has not been abused should be fundamentally sound. However, there are a few points to bear in mind, particularly in reference to the smaller-engined versions of the Mark 1. Beginning with the engine, smoke when starting up, particularly if the car has been idle for some time and again when accelerating hard, could mean that the oil seals on the valve stems have become brittle – by no means a rare occurrence on these smaller units. Their replacement is not a difficult task, but in most instances it will mean removing the cylinder head, although it is possible for the job to be done in situ with the aid of a special piece of kit to prevent the valves from dropping in. When looking around the outside of the engine, make sure there is no oil seepage between the head and the block because gasket replacement can be expensive.

The first Golf GTIs had an oil cooler mounted separately from the radiator, but when this was done away with the engine inevitably ran somewhat hotter. Do not be alarmed, therefore, if one of the later Mark 1s seems to be running on the hot side; this is quite normal. Conversely, some of the smaller Mark 1 engines tended to run hotter than the later units, and this could lead to a problem with the oil pump driveshaft, which could become rounded at the edges to the point where eventually the drive would be lost. In this event it is important to act very quickly to close down the engine once the oil pressure warning light comes on.

Trade in used performance Golfs and derivatives is usually brisk and supplies of cars in sound condition are normally plentiful. In 1992 this retailer in south-west London was selling more VWs than any other make.

In time, which could be after about 70 to 80,000 miles, the fuel injection equipment of an early Golf GTI is likely to clog up and cause erratic running. Unfortunately, a set of replacement injectors costs quite a lot of money, but the problem can be deferred by using an injector-cleaning additive in the fuel tank. Another potentially irritating item on both Mark 1 and Mark 2 carburettor-equipped cars is the automatic choke, which has been known to stick on the full-choke position on some occasions and refuse to operate at all on others; in consequence, many cars are now running around after having been converted to a manual choke.

Some Golfs, and GTIs in particular, have been given a much harder life than their external appearance may suggest, and excessive slop in the driveshafts is a pointer to this, as is a rumbling front wheel bearing (check for this by listening carefully while cornering briskly). Do not be too put off, however, if you discover some oil leakage from the axle gaiters because this is by no means rare and the gaiters are quite cheap to replace. While in this area of the car, check the front suspension struts, which should be free from oil leaks.

Clutches are cable-operated and a heavy pedal is an indication that the diaphragm has deteriorated and a replacement will soon be needed. On some of the Mark 1s the cable may even have pulled through and cracked the bulkhead, a problem which is less likely to be encountered on Mark 2s, which were reinforced in the bulkhead area. Another weak point on earlier cars is the lower mounting for the steering column, but it is easy enough to check on its condition; if it has broken there will be movement of the column and at the steering wheel rim as the clutch pedal is depressed.

Although gearboxes themselves tend to be robust, the linkages on early models left something to be desired and they do not take kindly to slovenly hand movements, especially when selecting reverse, when the lever should be depressed before, rather than whilst, making the necessary lateral movement. Habitual failure to do this can lead to the weakening of the reverse-gear protector so that, for example, when trying to move straight from fifth to second it is possible to find reverse instead. Any difficulty in selecting first or reverse gears from rest is another indication of a clutch problem.

A spongy brake pedal is a feature of right-hand-drive Mark 1s because the servo was retained in the same position as in left-hand-drive cars and had to be reached through a cross-shaft instead of being direct-acting. The problem is this shaft is inclined to flex. Reinforced conversion kits are available from various non-factory sources, but although these improve the situation they do not eradicate the brake pedal sponginess completely; the brake 'feel' was much improved on later cars. Be prepared for brake pad changes at regular intervals as they tend to wear fairly rapidly if the car is driven hard.

One of the few weak links of a Mark 2 Golf is the loss of synchromesh through the deterioration of the copper ring between first and second gears. The onset of trouble first manifests itself when the car has just been started and is still running cold, but as it gets worse the gearchange baulks even when everything has heated up. On higher-mileage cars this can be exacerbated by the breakdown of the oil seal between the clutch and gearbox, leading to contamination of the clutch. A typical mileage for this to happen is in the 35 to

The place to look for signs of mechanical neglect. The engine compartment should look as clean and tidy as this Mark 1 Golf GTI, which was photographed when it had already covered over 80,000 miles.

40,000 range, whereupon a replacement clutch is the obvious solution and quite a straightforward task.

Do not be put off if any of the more recent engines clatters noisily as soon as it is started up from cold; they nearly all do this after they have covered a few thousand miles. This is one of the penalties of the hydraulic tappets; when the crankshaft is turned over the oil takes a few seconds to be drawn up into the valve mechanism and by that time all the tappet clearances will have gone awry. Of course, they re-adjust themselves once they have become lubricated, but sometimes it can take a drive of three or four miles on a cold morning before the engine has completely quietened down again.

Around 1985 to 1987 (mainly B, C and D-registered cars on the UK market) there was a spate of problems with speedometers and odometers which from time to time either over-read, under-read or on occasions read nothing at all. As a result, a lot of cars from that period are now running on their second or subsequent speedometers. Usually, the tendency when seeing a car with an abnormally low mileage for its year is to assume that it has been 'clocked', but on these cars this

may well not be the case. However, an owner with foresight should have retained evidence of the car's genuine mileage at the time of a speedometer change, and in the case of a car with a full service record the truth should be easily verified.

As a general rule, there are usually sound reasons for selecting a car from towards the end of its production run rather than from the beginning, not only because by the time it was built any 'bugs' in the design will almost certainly have been eradicated, but also because the later cars will have had the benefit of the subtle changes in specification made in response to either user criticism or in-house routine R&D.

To quote a few examples, tall drivers in RHD markets should aim for one of the younger Golfs because on the earlier cars the wipers were unchanged from their normal left-hand-drive position and consequently they left an important segment of the screen unwiped ahead of the right-seated driver. If a GTI or one of the other fatter-tyred models is being sought, power-steering, which only became standard on the UK market during the last two years of the Mark 2, though previously it had been an optional extra, is highly desirable because otherwise the car's steering is heavy for tight-lock parking and manoeuvring. Late in 1987 for the 1988 season, the removal of the front-door quarterlights and the repositioning further forward of the rear-view mirrors was one of the most widely welcomed and practical detail changes made to the Mark 2 body.

A few words about the Convertible or, if you prefer, Cabriolet. Although some of these cars carry a GTI badge, which accurately identifies a fuel-injected engine, the suspension has never been as taut as that of a hatchback GTI, as a brisk trip through a series of S-bends will soon reveal. The open-topped cars were always intended for a somewhat gentler life and therefore should not be considered as candidates for setting new 'point to point' averages. Remember, too, that all convertibles without a targa-type roof tend to shake. The Golf probably shakes less than most, but it still shakes, and this has to be accepted as a price to pay for open-air driving. A legacy of the problem is that the welds which attach the steering rack mountings to the body structure can sometimes fail, but this is not as disastrous as it may sound because rewelding is a very straightforward job.

The cockpit of the car photographed on the previous page, again demonstrating that a properly cared for Golf should still be in thoroughly sound condition with 10 years of working life behind it.

Volkswagen can usually be relied upon to produce cars with durable upholstery. These front seats of a Golf Convertible showed little if any wear with the car in its eleventh year of service.

Although the basic shape of the Convertibles has remained the same, the cosmetic variations have proliferated and models such as the Clipper, Rivage and Sportline in their various forms will appeal or otherwise for subjective reasons. One constant, however, is that even the latest cars retain the original doors with quarterlights, which means that the door mirrors are mounted too far back for comfort (it was too costly an operation to re-engineer the door glasses without the support of a full window frame). Also on the question of rearward visibility, remember that on the earlier Convertibles the folded hood sat very high above the car's waistline, seriously impeding the view of the road behind. Later models folded somewhat more neatly.

The prospective buyer of a used Golf or derivative is confronted with an almost bewildering variety of models from which to choose. In addition to the many variations on the two Golf themes there have been almost as many varieties of Jettas, an abundance of different Sciroccos and already there have been several versions of the Corrado. As always, choice must be a subjective matter, but perhaps a few generalizations will be helpful.

Firstly, remember that the cost of ownership is probably more important than the initial purchase price. Therefore, having established your budget, aim to buy the best-maintained and lowest-mileage car you can find within it; depreciation, insurance premiums and routine running costs are expensive enough without having to carry the additional burden of avoidable repairs and replacement parts. In other words, do not be tempted into a higher-specification model that happens to fall within your purchase budget because it has some visible defects, has covered a higher than normal mileage, or has some questionable history; it will probably cost you a packet to keep going and then will not be worth the proverbial light when you are fed up with it and want to sell it.

At the same time it makes good sense to aim for a car with as full a specification as you can find within your budget; extras usually cost a lot when cars are new, but they tend to command a much lower price premium when the car is sold for a second or subsequent time. It has also been Volkswagen's policy to offer several grades of upholstery in a model range at any one time, and not only do the materials tend to be more durable towards the top end of the range, the more luxurious-looking seats are usually also found to be more supportive and comfortable.

When considering the practicalities of ownership, remember that the Golf hatches come in both three-door and five-door forms and have fold-down rear seats, so they can offer the useful combination of two-seat accommodation and extended luggage space, the Mark 2 being roomier in both respects than the Mark 1. On the other hand, both series of Jetta have a conventional luggage compartment of generous size, but without the Golf's fold-down seat versatility. For those who require only occasional rear seating, the two ranges of Scirocco offer a stylish alternative to their Golf counterparts, and these cars can often be picked up at very attractive prices compared with a Golf of similar age and specification, partly because they are classified one grade higher than the equivalent hatchback for insurance purposes. The Corrado, of course, is a much more expensive proposition, although quite high depreciation of the earlier examples – perhaps a reflection of the car's somewhat ponderous gearchange – has brought it within reach of a considerably larger secondhand market. Although a 2+2, the Corrado is, perhaps, best considered as a two-seater coupe with emergency extra accommodation.

With regard to the choice of engines for Golf GTIs, although the 1800, which became available on the Mark 1 from 1982, seems to be more popular than the 1600 version, partly because it tends to attract the same insurance premium, the smaller engine should not be underestimated. Being a shorter-stroke unit it revs more freely, and many people believe that the 1600 GTI is a more enjoyable car to drive. However, many cars which started out as a 1600 have subsequently been fitted with a replacement 1800 engine; the way to identify a genuine 1800 from one of these converted cars is to look for the computer, which was standard equipment on the 1800; it was much too complicated a job for one to be fitted at the time of an engine transplant.

An important question to consider when contemplating a Mark 2 GTI is whether to opt for the eight-valve or the 16-valve engine, each of which has its attractions. For the driver who likes to use the gearbox and an engine's full rev range, who is attracted by ultimate performance, the 16-valve is an understandable choice, but the eight-valve is no mean performer and its greater flexibility gives it the edge for anyone who does much of their mileage in urban areas in heavy traffic conditions. There are also two other points in favour of the eight-valve engine; most insurance companies rate it one class lower than the 16-valve, and maintenance costs are considerably lower bearing in mind the complexity of the top end of the 16-valve engine.

The prospective owner can be forgiven for feeling almost overwhelmed by the variety of choices of Golf and related cars, but one of the attractions of owning any of the cars discussed in this book is that they are well supported by owners' clubs, by informative and professionally produced journals and, for those who want to modify the standard product, by a wide variety of specialist tuning and accessory companies, some of whose products have full factory endorsement. Even clubs and journals with permanent offices move from time to time and have changes of personnel, but up-to-date club addresses can usually be found in the pages of the major classic car journals. Failing this, requests for information about their location and specific product advice should be addressed in the first instance to the public relations department of the Volkswagen company in the country concerned.

In the UK: V.A.G. (United Kingdom) Ltd, Yeomans Drive, Blakelands, Milton Keynes, MK14 5AN. Tel: 0908 679121.

In the USA: Volkswagen of America Inc, 3800 Hamlin Road, Auburn Hills, Michigan 48326. Tel: (313) 340 5000.

In Germany: Volkswagenwerke AG, 3180 Wolfsburg. Tel: 05361/90.

APPENDIX A

Technical specifications

Selected high-performance Golf, Jetta, Scirocco and Corrado models

Golf (USA Rabbit) GTI Mark 1 1600 – produced 1976 to 1983

Style: Based on standard Golf 3-door hatchback body with prominent body side mouldings, wider wheels and tyres and special grille and tail badging. Only available in UK with LHD or with after-sales RHD conversion until factory RHD version introduced in July 1979. 5-door body available in some markets from 1981. (Golf Mark 1 3-door and 5-door hatchbacks also available in different markets in a variety of specifications with choice of 1.1, 1.3, 1.5 or 1.6-litre carburettor-fed petrol engines and 1.6-litre diesel or turbodiesel.)

Engine: Transverse-mounted 4-cyl, toothed belt-driven sohc, alloy cylinder-head, cast-iron block, 79.5 x 80.0mm, 1,588cc (3.13 x 3.15in, 96.9cu in), CR 9.5:1. Bosch K-Jetronic fuel injection. Maximum power 110bhp (81kW) at 6,100rpm. Maximum torque 101lb/ft (137.3Nm) at 5,000rpm. USA: CR 8.5:1. 91bhp (67kW) at 5,500rpm. Maximum torque 98lb/ft (135Nm) at 3,000rpm.

Transmission: Front-wheel drive. Diaphragm single-plate clutch and 4-speed all-synchromesh gearbox until 1981, 5-speed from 1981 and in USA. Final-drive ratio 3.7:1 (4-speed), 3.9:1 (5-speed). Gearbox ratios (4-speed) 3.45. 1.94, 1.37, 0.97, reverse 3.17:1, 17.3mph/1,000rpm in top gear; (5-speed) 3.45, 2.12, 1.44, 1.13, 0.91, reverse 3.17:1, 18.5mph/1,000rpm in top gear.

Suspension, steering and brakes: Front, independent with MacPherson struts, lower wishbones, coil springs and anti-rollbar. Rear, semi-independent with trailing arms, torsion beam, coil springs, telescopic dampers and anti-rollbar. Rack-and-pinion steering, 3.3 turns lock to lock, servo-assisted in USA. 9.4in (239mm) ventilated front disc brakes, 7.1in (226mm) rear drum brakes, vacuum servo. 175/70HR-13 radial-ply tyres on 5½in-rim steel wheels, similar-size alloy wheels optional. USA: 185/60HR-14 tyres on 6in-rim wheels.

Dimensions: Wheelbase 7ft 10.5in (240cm); front track 4ft 7.3in (140.5cm), USA 4ft 6.7in (139cm); rear track 4ft 5.9in (137cm), USA 4ft 5.5in (136mm). Overall length 12ft 2.5in (372cm), USA 12ft 11.3in (394.5cm); width 5ft 3.5in (161cm), USA 5ft 4.2in (163cm); height 4ft 6.9in (139.5cm), USA 4ft 7.5in (141cm). Typical unladen weight 1,720lb (780kg) rising to 1,851lb (840kg).

Typical UK retail price when new: £3,372 in 1976.

Jetta GLi Mark 1 1600 – produced from 1979 to 1982

As Golf GTI Mark 1 1600 except:

Style: Based on standard Jetta 2-door and 4-door bodywork derived from Golf hatchback design with separate rear luggage compartment. Different front-end styling incorporating rectangular headlamps. GLi only available as 4-door in UK. (Jetta Mark 1 2-door and 4-door saloons also available in different markets in a variety of specifications with choice of 1.1, 1.3, 1.5 or 1.6-litre carburettor-fed petrol engines and 1.6-litre diesel or turbodiesel.)

Dimensions: Overall length 13ft 9.1in (419.5cm); width 5ft 4.2in (163cm); height 4ft 7.5in (141cm). Typical unladen weight: 2-door 1,906lb (865kg), 4-door 1,962lb (890kg).

Typical UK retail price when new: £5,980 in 1980.

Golf GTI Mark 1 1800 – produced 1982 to 1984

As Golf GTI Mark 1 1600 except:
Style: Additional 1984 special edition offered in UK with twin-headlamp grille, metal sunroof and sports wheels standard.
Engine: Bore x stroke 81.0 x 86.4mm, 1,781cc (3.19 x 3.40in, 108.7cu in), CR 10:1. Maximum power 112bhp (82.5kW) at 5,800rpm. Maximum torque 109lb/ft (153Nm) at 3,500rpm.
Transmission: Final-drive ratio 3.65:1. Gearbox ratios as Mark 1 1600 5-speed, 19.8mph/1,000rpm in top gear.
UK retail price when new: £6,500 in 1982.

Jetta GLi Mark 1 1800 – produced 1982 to 1983

As Jetta GLi Mark 1 1600 except:
Engine: As Golf GTI 1800.

Golf GTI Mark 2 1800 – produced 1984 to 1991

Style: Based on standard Golf Mark 2 3-door and 5-door hatchback bodies with Mark 1-type badging and red bumper inserts and grille surround. Modified front and rear valances, wheelarch extensions and body side mouldings from late 1989. (Golf Mark 2 3-door and 5-door hatchbacks also offered in different markets in a variety of specifications with choice of 1.1, 1.3, 1.5, 1.6 or 1.8-litre carburettor-fed petrol engines and 1.6-litre diesel or turbo diesel.)
Engine: Bore x stroke 81.0 x 86.4mm, 1,781cc (3.19 x 3.40in, 108.7cu in), CR 10:1. Digifant electronic fuel injection. Maximum power 112bhp (82.5kW) DIN at 5,400rpm. Maximum torque 114lb/ft (158Nm) at 3,500/4,000rpm. USA: 107bhp (79kW) at 5,400rpm. Maximum torque 113.5lb/ft (157Nm) at 3,800rpm.
Transmission: Front-wheel drive. Diaphragm single-plate clutch and 5-speed all-synchromesh gearbox. Final-drive ratio 3.67:1. Gearbox ratios 3.46, 2.12, 1.44, 1.13, 0.89, reverse 3.17:1, 20.1mph/1,000rpm in top gear.
Suspension, steering and brakes: Front, independent with MacPherson struts, lower wishbones, coil springs and anti-rollbar. Rear, semi-independent with trailing arms, torsion beam, coil springs, telescopic dampers and anti-rollbar. Rack-and-pinion steering, 3.75 turns lock to lock, optional power assistance, 3.2 turns lock to lock. 9.4in (239mm) ventilated front disc brakes, 8.9in (226mm) solid rear disc brakes, vacuum servo. 175/70HR-13 radial-ply tyres on 5½in-rim steel wheels on 3-door, 185/60HR-14 radial-ply tyres on 6in-rim alloy wheels on 5-door and optional for 3-door.
Dimensions: Wheelbase 8ft 1.4in (247cm); front track 4ft 8.2in (143cm); rear track 4ft 8in (142cm). Overall length 13ft 0.9in (398.5cm); width 5ft 6.1in (168cm); height 4ft 7.5in (141cm). Typical unladen weight (3-door) 2,028lb (920kg), (5-door) 2,072lb (940kg).
UK retail price when new: (3-door) £7,867 in 1984, (5-door) £8,910 in 1985.

Jetta GT Mark 2 – produced 1984 to 1991

As Golf GTI Mark 2 except:
Style: Based on standard Jetta 2-door and 4-door bodywork derived from Golf hatchback design with separate rear luggage compartment. Different front-end styling incorporating rectangular headlamps. (Jetta Mark 2 2-door and 4-door saloons also offered from 1984 in different markets in a variety of specifications with choice of 1.3, 1.5, 1.6 or 1.8-litre carburettor-fed petrol engines and 1.6-litre diesel or turbo diesel.)
Dimensions: Overall length 14ft 2in (432cm); width 5ft 6in (168cm); height 4ft 8in (142cm). Typical unladen weight (4-door) 2,138lb (970kg).
UK retail price when new: £8,497 in 1986.

Golf GTI Mark 2 16V – produced 1985 to 1991

As Golf GTI Mark 2 1800 except:
Style: Foglamps built into front spoiler.
Engine: 2ohc, exhaust camshaft driven by toothed belt, then inlet camshaft by chain, 16 valves, hydraulic tappets. Bosch KA-Jetronic mechanical fuel injection. Maximum power 139bhp (102kW) at 6,100rpm. Maximum torque 133lb/ft (168Nm) at

4,600rpm. USA: Maximum power 129bhp (95kW) at 5,800rpm. Maximum torque 133lb/ft (168Nm) at 4,250rpm.
Transmission: 5th gear ratio 0.91:1, 19.7mph/1,000rpm in top gear.
Suspension, steering and brakes: 10.1in ventilated front disc brakes. 185/60-14 radial-ply tyres on 6in-rim alloy wheels standard on 3-door, 185/55VR-15 tyres on 6in-rim BBS alloy wheels on all 16V models from late 1989.
Dimensions: Height 4ft 6.9in (139.5cm). Typical unladen weight (3-door) 2,116lb (960kg), (5-door) 2,160lb (980kg).
UK retail price when new: (3-door) £10,894 in 1986, (5-door) £14,449 in 1990.

Jetta GTi 16V Mark 2 – produced 1987 to 1991

As Jetta GT Mark 2 except:
Engine: As Golf GTI Mark 2 16V.
Dimensions: Typical unladen weight 2,227lb (1,010kg).
UK retail price when new: £11,998 in 1987.

Golf GTI G60 – produced from 1990 to 1991

As 3-door and 5-door Golf GTI Mark 2 1800 except:
Engine: 1,781cc sohc equipped with double belt-driven G-lader supercharger with intercooler and running at 1.6 times engine speed. CR 8:1. Digifant fuel injection. Maximum power 160bhp (118kW) at 5,800rpm. Maximum torque 166lb/ft (225Nm) at 3,800rpm.
Transmission: Final-drive ratio 3.68:1. Gearbox ratios 3.78, 2.12, 1.34, 0.97, 0.76:1.
Suspension, steering and brakes: Ride height lowered by further 10mm, uprated dampers, 23mm front and 21mm rear anti-rollbars. Electronic ABS braking standard, ventilated discs all round. 185/55R-15V tyres on 6in-rim alloy wheels or 195/50R-15V tyres on 6½in-rim alloy wheels.
Dimensions: Front track 4ft 8.4in (143cm); rear track 4ft 8.2in (143cm). Overall length 13ft 3in (404cm); width 5ft 6.9in (170cm); height 4ft 7.3in (140.5cm). Typical unladen weight (3-door) 2,380lb (1,080kg), (5-door) 2,435lb (1,105kg).
UK retail price when new: £15,967 in 1991.

Rallye Golf – produced 1989

As Golf GTI G60 except:
Style: LHD 3-door saloon produced in 5,000 homologation run for motorsport use. Wider wheelarches and body side panels, front and rear bumpers with integral aprons, different radiator grille incorporating broad-beam DE headlamps.
Engine: 80.6 x 86.4mm, 1,763cc. CR 8:1. Power and torque as G60 1,781cc engine.
Transmission: Syncro permanent 4wd incorporating viscous coupling, modified Passat 5-speed gearbox.
Suspension, steering and brakes: 205/50R-15V tyres on 6in-rim 15in alloy wheels.
Dimensions: Front track 4ft 8.3in (143cm); rear track 4ft 8.5in (143cm). Overall length 13ft 2.9in (403.5cm); width 5ft 8.9in (170cm); height 4ft 7.1in (140cm). Typical unladen weight 2,634lb (1,195kg).
UK retail price when new: £16,940 in 1989.

Scirocco GLi/GTI Mark 1 – produced 1976 to 1981

Style: Based on standard Scirocco 3-door 4-seater hatchback coupe body with twin headlamps, wider wheels with lower-profile tyres and different tail badging. More rounded grille, lights clusters and bumpers from 1977. (Scirocco Mark 1 3-door coupe also offered from 1974 in different markets in a variety of specifications with choice of 1.1, 1.3, 1.5 and 1.6-litre carburettor-fed petrol engines.)
Engine: Transverse-mounted 4-cyl, toothed belt-driven sohc, alloy cylinder-head, cast-iron block, 79.5 x 80.0mm, 1,588cc (3.13 x 3.15in, 96.9cu in), CR 9.5:1. Bosch K-Jetronic fuel injection. Maximum power 110bhp (81kW) DIN at 6,100rpm. Maximum torque 101lb/ft (137.3Nm) at 5,000rpm.
Transmission: Front-wheel drive. Diaphragm single-plate clutch and 4-speed all-synchromesh gearbox until 1979, 5-speed thereafter. Final-drive ratio 3.67:1. Gearbox ratios (4-speed) 3.46, 1.94, 1.37, 0.97, reverse 3.17:1, 17.3mph/1,000rpm in top gear; (5-speed) 3.45, 2.12, 1.44, 1.13, 0.91, reverse 3.17:1, 18.5mph/1,000rpm in top gear.

Suspension, steering and brakes: Front, independent with MacPherson struts, lower wishbones, coil springs and anti-rollbar. Rear, semi-independent with trailing arms, torsion beam, coil springs, telescopic dampers and anti-rollbar. Rack-and-pinion steering, 3.3 turns lock to lock. 9.4in (239mm) ventilated front disc brakes, 7.1in (226mm) rear drum brakes, vacuum servo. 175/70HR-13 radial-ply tyres on 5½in-rim steel wheels, similar-size alloy wheels optional.
Dimensions: Wheelbase 7ft 10.5in (240cm); front track 4ft 7.3in (140.5cm); rear track 4ft 5.9in (137cm). Overall length 12ft 7.8in (385.5cm), USA 12ft 11.7in (395.5cm); width 5ft 4.0in (162.5cm); height 4ft 3.6in (131cm). Typical unladen weight 1,763lb (800kg).
UK retail price when new: £6,304 in 1979.

Scirocco GTI, GLi, GTX Mark 2 1600 and 1800 – produced 1981 to 1992

Style: Based on standard Mark 2 3-door 4-seater Scirocco coupe body with different badging and additional equipment. (Scirocco Mark 2 3-door coupe also offered in different markets in a variety of specifications with choice of 1.3, 1.6 and 1.8-litre carburettor-fed petrol engines.)
Engine: Transverse-mounted 4-cyl, toothed belt-driven sohc, alloy cylinder-head, cast-iron block, 79.5 x 80.0mm, 1,588cc (3.13 x 3.15in, 96.9cu in), CR 9.5:1. Bosch K-Jetronic fuel injection. Maximum power 110bhp (81kW) DIN at 6,100rpm. Maximum torque 101lb/ft (140Nm) at 5,000rpm. From 1982: Bore x stroke 81.0 x 86.4mm, 1,781cc (3.19 x 3.40in, 108.7cu in), CR 10:1. Maximum power 112bhp (82.5kW) DIN at 5,800rpm. Maximum torque 109lb/ft (153Nm) at 3,500rpm. USA: 79.5 x 86.4mm, 1,716cc (3.13 x 3.40in, 104.7cu in). CR 8.2:1. Maximum power 75bhp (55kW) at 5,000rpm. Maximum torque 89lb/ft (122Nm) at 3,000rpm. Later, 1,781cc engine, details as Golf 2.
Transmission: Front-wheel drive. Diaphragm single-plate clutch and 5-speed all-synchromesh gearbox. Final-drive ratio 3.89:1 or 3.7:1. Gearbox ratios 3.45. 2.18, 1.44, 1.13, 0.91, reverse 3.17:1, 18.5mph/1,000rpm in top gear.
Suspension, steering and brakes: Front, independent with MacPherson struts, lower wishbones, coil springs and anti-rollbar. Rear, semi-independent with trailing arms, torsion beam, coil springs, telescopic dampers and anti-rollbar. Rack-and-pinion steering, 3.3 turns lock to lock, servo-assisted in USA. 9.4in (239mm) ventilated front disc brakes, 7.1in (226mm) rear drum brakes, vacuum servo. 175/70HR-13 radial-ply tyres on 5½in-rim alloy wheels.
Dimensions: Wheelbase 7ft 10.5in (240cm); front track 4ft 7.3in (140.5cm); rear track 4ft 5.9in (137cm). Overall length 13ft 3.5in (405cm), USA 13ft 9.8in (421cm); width 5ft 4.0in (162.5cm); height 4ft 3.4in (130.5cm). Typical unladen weight (GTX) 2,029lb (920kg).
UK retail price when new: £7,125 (GTI) in 1982.

Scirocco GTX 16V Mark 2 – produced 1985 to 1992

As Scirocco GTX Mark 2 1800 except:
Style: '16V' badges on grille, centre pillars and rear, twin exhaust pipes.
Suspension, steering and brakes: Rear disc brakes.
Engine: As Golf GTI 16V.
Dimensions: Typical unladen weight 2,646lb (1,200kg).
UK retail price when new: £10,960 in 1986.

Golf (USA Rabbit) Convertible GLi and GTi – produced from 1979

As Golf GTI Mark 1 1600 and 1800 except:
Style: 2-door 4-seater open-top body by Karmann based on standard Golf 3-door Mark 1 body with structural strengthening including permanent roll-over hoop. GLi designation changed to GTi in 1983 with upgraded interior specification. Power hood standard from 1989. Rabbit identifiable by more substantial impact-resisting bumpers and front and rear indicator lights on body sides. (Golf Cabriolet also offered with choice of 1.5, 1.6 and 1.8-litre carburettor-fed petrol engines.)
Engine: USA (1800): CR 9:1. Maximum power 95bhp (70kW) at 5,500rpm. Maximum torque 103lb/ft (142Nm) at 3,000rpm.
Transmission: Final-drive ratio 3.895:1, 19.7mph/1,000rpm in top gear.

Suspension, steering and brakes: USA: No rear anti-rollbar. Rear drum brakes. 175/70HR-13 tyres on 5½in-rim alloy wheels.

Dimensions: Overall length 12ft 6.2in (381.5cm), 12ft 6.9in (383cm) from 1983; height 4ft 6.9in (139.5cm). Typical unladen weight 2,072lb (940kg), 1988 2,193lb (995kg), USA 2,237lb (1,015kg).

UK retail price when new: (GTi) £8,692 in 1980, (GTi Sportline) £16,143 in 1991.

Corrado 16V – produced from 1989

Style: 3-door 2+2 sports coupe body with adjustable rear spoiler

Engine: Until 1992 as Golf GTI 16V. CR 10:1. Maximum power 136bhp (102kW) at 6,300rpm. Maximum torque 119lb/ft (165Nm) at 4,800rpm. From 1992 82.5 x 92.8mm, 1,984cc, CR 10.8:1. Maximum power 136bhp (102kW) at 5,800rpm. Maximum torque 132lb/ft (182Nm) at 4,400rpm.

Transmission: Front-wheel drive. Diaphragm single-plate clutch and 5-speed all-synchromesh gearbox. Final-drive ratio 3.68:1. Gearbox ratios until 1992 3.40, 2.12, 1.44, 1.13, 0.91, reverse 3.80:1, 20.7mph/1,000rpm in top gear, from 1992 3.78, 2.21, 1.43, 1.03, 0.84, reverse 3.80:1, 22.4mph/1,000rpm in top gear.

Suspension, steering and brakes: Front, independent with MacPherson struts, lower wishbones, anti-rollbar, negative-offset steering. Rear, semi-independent with torsion beam trailing arms with track-correcting bearings, anti-rollbar. Rack-and-pinion steering, 3.17 turns lock to lock. 10in (254mm) disc brakes all round, ventilated at front, ABS standard. 195/50VR-15 radial-ply tyres on 6in-rim alloy wheels.

Dimensions: Wheelbase 8ft 1.2in (247cm); front track 4ft 8.5in (143.5cm); rear track 4ft 8.2in (143cm). Overall length 13ft 3.3in (405cm); width 5ft 5.9in (167cm); height 4ft 3.9in (132cm).

Typical unladen weight 2,426lb (1,100kg).

UK retail price when new: £16,699 in 1989, £17,192 in 1992.

Corrado G60 – produced from 1989

As Corrado 16V except:

Engine: Based on 1,781cc sohc Golf GTI engine but equipped with Volkswagen-developed G60 supercharger mechanically driven from crankshaft. Multi-point electronic fuel injection and fully electronic ignition. CR 8:1. Maximum power 160bhp (118kW) DIN at 5,600rpm. Maximum torque 165lb/ft (225Nm) at 4,000rpm.

Transmission: Final-drive ratio 3.68:1. Gearbox ratios 3.78, 2.12, 1.34, 0.97, 0.76, reverse 3.80:1. 23.9mph/1,000rpm in top gear.

Suspension, steering and brakes: ABS brakes standard (LHD), 280mm ventilated front discs, 226mm solid rear discs.

Dimensions: Typical unladen weight 2,459lb (1,115kg).

UK retail price when new: £19,338 in 1989, £18,509 in 1992.

Corrado VR6 – produced from 1992

As Corrado 16V except:

Engine: Transverse-mounted VR6 15deg V6-cyl sohc with cast-iron block and alloy cylinder heads, 82 x 90.3mm, 2,861cc (3.23 x 3.56in, 174.5cu in). Bosch Motronic fuel injection, electronic ignition. CR 10:1. Maximum power 190bhp (142kW) at 5,800rpm. Maximum torque 181lb/ft (250Nm) at 4,200rpm.

Transmission: Final-drive ratio 3.39:1. Gearbox ratios 3.78, 2.12, 1.46, 1.03, 0.84:1, 24.3mph/1,000rpm in top gear.

Suspension, steering and brakes: 280mm ventilated front brake discs, 226mm solid rear discs. Electronic traction control linked to front brakes. 205/50R-15V tyres on 6½in-rim 15in alloy wheels.

Dimensions: Typical unladen weight 2,733lb (1,240kg).

UK retail price when new: £19,895 in 1992.

PRINCIPAL FOUR-CYLINDER ENGINES FOR VW GOLF MARKS 1 AND 2 AND DERIVATIVES

Petrol

1,093cc (69.5 x 72mm) 50bhp/37kW (from 1981)
1,093cc (69.5 x 72mm) 52bhp/38kW (from 1974)
1,272cc (69.5 x 72mm) 55bhp/40.5kW (from 1983)
1,272cc (75 x 72mm) 60bhp/44kW (from 1979)
1,457cc (79.5 x 73.4mm) 63bhp/46.5kW (from 1979)
1,457cc (79.5 x 73.4mm) 70bhp/51.5kW (from 1977)
1,471cc (76.5 x 80mm) 70bhp/52kW (from 1974)
1,471cc (76.5 x 80mm) 85bhp/64kW (from 1974)
1,588cc (79.5 x 80mm) 75bhp/55kW (from 1975)
1,588cc (79.5 x 80mm) 77bhp/56.5kW (from 1979)
1,588cc (79.5 x 80mm) 75bhp/55kW (from 1975)
1,588cc (79.5 x 80mm) 110bhp/81kW (from 1975)
1,595cc (81 x 77.4mm) 72bhp/53kW (from 1986)
1,595cc (81 x 77.4mm) 75bhp/55kW (from 1986)
1,716cc (79.5 x 86.4mm) 66bhp/48.5kW (from 1979)
1,716cc (79.5 x 86.4mm) 75bhp/55kW (from 1979)
1,781cc (81 x 86.4mm) 91bhp/67kW (from 1983)
1,781cc (81 x 86.4mm) 90bhp/66kW (from 1983)
1,781cc (81 x 86.4mm) 107bhp/78.5kW (from 1986)
1,781cc (81 x 86.4mm) 112bhp/82.5kW (from 1982)
1,781cc (81 x 86.4mm) 129bhp/95kW (from 1986)
1,781cc (81 x 86.4mm) 139bhp/102kW (from 1983)

Diesel

1,471cc (76.5 x 80mm) 50bhp/37kW (from 1976)
1,588cc (79.5 x 80mm) 54bhp/39.5kW (from 1980)
1,588cc (79.5 x 80mm) 70bhp/51.5kW (from 1981)

MANUAL GEARBOX RATIOS FOR GOLFS AND DERIVATIVES

Four-speed

3.454, 2.05, 1.347, 0.963, rev 3.384:1
3.45, 1.94, 1.29 or 1.37, 0.88 or 0.91 or 0.97, rev 3.17:1
3.45, 1.77, 1.04, 0.80, rev 3.38:1
3.45, 1.75, 1.06, 0.70, rev 3.17:1
3.45, 1.95, 1.25, 0.89, rev 3.38:1
3.45, 1.77, 1.08, 0.80, rev 3.38:1
3.78, 2.12, 1.34, 0.97, 0.76:1

Five-speed

3.40, 2.12, 1.44, 1.13, 0.91, rev 3.80:1
3.45, 1.94, 1.29 or 1.37, 0.91 or 0.97, 0.71 or 0.76, rev 3.17:1
3.45, 2.118, 1.444, 1.129, 0.89 or 0.912, rev 3.17:1
3.45, 1.95, 1.25, 0.89, 0.74, rev 3.38:1
3.78, 2.12, 1.34, 0.97, 0.80, rev 3.80:1
3.78, 2.12, 1.46, 1.03, 0.84:1

Final-drive ratios

3.38, 3.68, 3.895, 3.94, 4.06, 4.17, 4.267, 4.47, 4.57, 4.86:1

UK registrations by model and year, 1982–1991

GOLF 1

1982

All models	26311
3-door	11915
5-door	14396
N	14
L	23
LS	1
GLS	32
Diesel	10
C	7028
C Diesel	2084
C Formel E	3502
CL	4812
GL	3940
GTI	2914
GTI 1.8	916
Cabriolet GL	524
Cabriolet GLi	384
Convertible GLi 1.8	123
Convertible GLS	4

1983

All models	25764
C	4700
C Diesel	1168
C Formel E	2414
CL	1811
GL	2034
GX	2165
Driver	4246
GTI	42
GTI 1.8	6106
Cabriolet GL	309
Cabriolet GLi	24
Cabriolet GTI	491
Convertible GLi 1.8	254

1984

All models	2734
Driver	204
GX	90
C	1034
CL	21
GL	67
GTI 1.8	152
Cabriolet GL	229
Convertible GLi	447
Cabriolet GTI	490

1985

All models	1294
Driver	9
GX	2
C	18
CL	8
GL	208
GTI 1.8	1
Cabriolet GL	293
Convertible GLi	14
Cabriolet GTI	741

GOLF 2

1984

All models	21516
standard	464
C	7300
CL	6082
GL	3937
GTI	3733

1985

All models	29851
standard	121
Match	1188
C	10222
CL	7222
GL	4546
GL 1.8	588
GTI	5955
Convertible CC	9

1986

All models	35773
standard	1
C	9260
CL	10918
GL	5557
Driver	12
Match	1
GTI	9126
GTI 16V	220
Cabriolet	36

Cabriolet GL	174
Convertible CC	468

1987

All models	40543
standard	807
C	9442
CL	9604
GL	5014
Driver	2454
GTI	8427
GTI 16V	3135
Syncro	1
Cabriolet	209
Cabriolet GL	2
Cabriolet Clipper	611
Cabriolet GTI	834
Convertible CC	3

1988

All models	51400
standard	12545
C	733
CL	14498
GL	5057
Driver	708
Tour	2458
GTI	10512
GTI 16V	3051
Syncro	75
Cabriolet	1
Cabriolet Clipper	710
Cabriolet GTI	1052

1989

All models	56055
standard	11172
C	2830
CL	7314
GL	4690
Driver	10415
Tour	32
GTI	11865
GTI 16V	4190
Syncro	398
Rallye 4x4	5
Cabriolet Clipper	1427
Cabriolet GTI	1138

1990

All models	47729
standard	12810
CL	4391
GL	3743
GTD Turbo	136
Driver	11785
Tour	3
GTI	8961
GTI 16V	3285
GTI G60	3
Syncro	166
Rallye 4x4	57
Cabriolet Clipper	1253
Cabriolet GTI	1136

1991

All models	33862
standard	3334
Ryder	5125
CL	773
GL	1689
GTD Turbo	1265
Driver	11639
GTI	6164
GTI 16V	2102
GTI G60	3
Syncro	35
Rallye 4x4	3
GTI Sportline	156
GTI Rivage	260
Cabriolet GTI	337
Cabriolet Clipper	977

JETTA 1

1982

All models	7937
C	5169
L	22
LS 1.5	61
GLS 1.5	2
CL	1754
GL	914
GLi	1
Others	14

1983

All models	7726
C	3405
LX	517
CL	1260
GL	943

1984

All models	2230
C	727
LX	883
CL	72
GL	548

1985

All models	28
C	12
CL	2
GL	14

JETTA 2

1984

All models	2031
C	819
CL	584
GL	474
GLX	154

1985

All models	5801
C	2375
CL	2188
GL	1004
GLX	99
TX	135

1986

All models	6774
C	2136
CL	576
GL	666
GLX	3
TX	2744
GT	649

1987

All models	6948
standard	117
C	2269
CL	291
GL	722
TX	2557
GT	495
GTi	497

1988

All models	7596
standard	1545
C	984
CL	2
GL	934
TX	3057
GT	1
GTi	508
GTi 16V	558
Syncro	7

1989

All models	7230
standard	2031
CL	301
GL	1334
TX	2963
GTi	339
GTi 16V	219
Syncro	43

1990

All models	6118
standard	1729
LX	35
GX	132
TX	2644
GL	1139
GTi	228
GTi 16V	151
Syncro	60

1991

All models	3623
standard	293
LX	555
GL	619
GX	1688
TX	298
GTi	101
GTi 16V	64
Syncro	5

SCIROCCO 2

1982
All models	7215
CL	1438
GL	4011
GTi	1470
GTi 1.8	296

1983
All models	6807
CL	2179
GL	2763
GTi17	
GTi 1.8	1848

1984
All models	5929
CL	1523
GL	1946
GT	257
GTL	153
GTX	220
Storm	479

GTi 1.8	1351

1985
All models	5653
CL	25
GL	77
GT	1777
GTL	967
GTX	1675
GTS	984
Storm	99
GTi 1.8	49

1986
All models	5704
GT	3411
GTL	3
GTX	1540
GTX 16V	7
GTi 1.8	1
GTS	742

1987
All models	5094

GT	2927
GTX	965
GTX 16V	3
GTS	18
Scala	1181

1988
All models	4569
GT	1961
GTX	773
Scala	1835

1989
All models	3699
GT	2177
GTX	58
Scala	1464

1990
All models	2863
GT	1812
GTX	3
Scala	1048

1991
All models	1221
GT	940
Scala	281

CORRADO

1989
All models	371
16V	370
G60 LHD	1

1990
All models	1623
16V	1614
G60 LHD	8
G60 RHD	1

1991
All models	1803
16V	753
16V 2-litre	3
G60 LHD	2
G60 RHD	1045

UK REGISTRATIONS BY MODEL, 1982–1991

	GOLF 1	GOLF 2	JETTA 1	JETTA 2	SCIROCCO 2	CORRADO
1982	26311		7937		7215	
1983	25764		7726		6807	
1984	2734	21516	2230	2031	5929	
1985	1294	29851	28	5801	5653	
1986		35773		6774	5704	
1987		40543		6948	5094	
1988		51400		7596	4569	
1989		56055		7230	3699	371
1990		47729		6118	2863	1623
1991		33862		3623	1221	1803
TOTAL	56103	316729	17921	46121	48754	3797

MILESTONES OF GOLF 1 AND 2 PRODUCTION HISTORY

May 1974 – International press launch of Golf in Munich.
March 1976 – 500,000th Golf built.
June 1976 – International press launch of Golf GTI in Frankfurt.
September 1976 – International press launch of Golf Diesel in Stockholm.
October 1976 – 1,000,000th Golf built.
June 1978 – 2,000,000th Golf built.
March 1979 – International press launch of Golf Convertible in St Tropez.
August 1979 – Introduction of plastic bumpers and five-speed gearbox for GTI.
September 1979 – 3,000,000th Golf built.
August 1980 – Styling changes including larger rear light clusters, modified dashboard; diesel engine increased from 1.5 to 1.6 litres, 4+E manual gearbox.
November 1980 – 4,000,000th Golf built.
January 1981 – International press launch of Formel E package at Eibsee.
February 1982 – 5,000,000th Golf built.
March 1982 – International press launch of Golf Turbodiesel in Ingolstadt.
August 1982 – Introduction of 1.8-litre engine in Golf GTI.
August 1983 – International press launch of Golf 2 in Munich.
September 1983 – 6,000,000th Golf built; Golf 2 on sale.
January 1984 – Introduction of Golf 2 GTI.
August 1984 – Introduction of 1.8-litre injection engine with controlled catalyst.
January 1985 – Uprated GTI including twin headlights, twin exhaust pipes and new interior trim.
March 1985 – 7,000,000th Golf built.
August 1985 – Introduction of low-maintenance technology including hydraulic tappets, electronic ignition and extended service intervals.
March 1986 – Introduction of Golf GTI 16V with 1.8-litre engine.
April 1986 – Introduction of Golf Syncro with 4wd and 1.8-litre engine.
May 1986 – 8,000,000th Golf built.
August 1986 – Uprated Golf CL and GL; new interior trim; introduction of Golf GT; ABS braking for Golf Syncro.

February 1987 – Introduction of optional ABS for Golf GT, GTI and GTI 16V.
March 1987 – Introduction of 1.6-litre engine with electronically controlled carburettor and controlled catalyst.
May 1987 – Introduction of 1.3-litre engine with Digijet injection system and controlled catalyst.
June 1987 – 9,000,000th Golf built.
August 1987 – Major detail changes including new radiator grille, rubbing strips, deleted quarter-windows, relocated mirrors, new interior trim and steering wheels; introduction of Golf GT Syncro with standard ABS.
November 1987 – Introduction of 1.8-litre Golf GT Special.
January 1988 – Introduction of Golf Rallye G60 with syncro drive and supercharged 1.8-litre engine.
June 1988 – 10,000,000th Golf built
August 1989 – Improved equipment; CL now base model, new bumpers for GL and GTI; introduction of 1.6-litre Turbodiesel.
October 1989 – 11,000,000th Golf built.
November 1989 – Introduction of 1.6-litre catalyst diesel.
January 1990 – Introduction of Golf Country with syncro drive.
February 1990 – Controlled catalyst standard on all Golfs; introduction of Golf GTI G60 with supercharged 1.8-litre engine.
November 1990 – 12,000,000th Golf built.
August 1991 – International press launch of Golf 3 in Munich after 12,700,000 Golfs 1 and 2 built.

THE FIRST 10,000,000 GOLFS

Of the total production of the first 10 million cars, 6.4 million were Mark 1s and 3.4 million Mark 2s. Total diesel and turbodiesel production amounted to 2,560,000 cars, there had been 790,000 GTIs, 230,000 convertibles and 160,000 pickups (known as the Caddy in the UK). Exports had totalled 6.4 million cars, the top 12 markets being:

United States	1,750,000	Austria	290,000
Italy	860,000	Switzerland	255,000
France	640,000	Belgium	255,000
Great Britain	365,000	South Africa	210,000
Mexico	325,000	Canada	205,000
Netherlands	325,000	Japan	145,000

APPENDIX C

Product identification by year, range and model

GOLF 1: 3dr and 5dr saloons, 1.1, 1.5, 1.6 and 1.8 engines, 1974 to 1983

JETTA 1: 2dr and 4dr saloons, 1.1, 1.5, 1.6 and 1.8 engines

SCIROCCO 1: 3dr coupes, 1.1, 1.5, 1.6 and 1.8 engines, 1974 to 1981

GOLF 2: 3dr and 5dr saloons, 1.3, 1.6 and 1.8 engines, 1983 to 1991

JETTA 2: 2dr and 4dr saloons, 1.3, 1.6 and 1.8 engines, 1983 to 1991

SCIROCCO 2: 3dr coupes, 1.3, 1.6 and 1.8 engines, 1981 to 1992

GOLF CONVERTIBLE/CABRIOLET: 2dr, 1.3, 1.6 and 1.8 engines, 1981-on

CORRADO: 2dr coupes, 1.8, 2.0 and 2.7 engines, 1989-on

Golf 1 1.1 1974–81
Golf 1 C 1.1 1981–3
Golf 1 C 1.3 1981–3
Golf 1 C 1.5 1981–3
Golf 1 L 1.1 1974–81
Golf 1 CL 1.1 1981–3
Golf 1 CL 1.3 1981–3
Golf 1 CL 1.5 1981–3
Golf 1 S 1.5 1974–5, 1977–81
Golf 1 LS 1.5 1974–5, 1977–81
Golf 1 S 1.6 1975–7
Golf 1 S 1.3 1979–81
Golf 1 LS 1.6 1975–7
Golf 1 LS 1.3 1979–81
Golf 1 GTI 1.6 1975–82
Golf 1 GTI 1.8 1982–3
Golf 1 Diesel 1.5 1976–80
Golf 1 Diesel 1.6 1980–82
Golf 1 C, CL & GL Diesel 1.6 1982–3
Golf 1 C, CL, GL & GTD Turbodiesel
  1.6 1982–3
Golf 1 GL 1.1 1977–81
Golf 1 GL 1.3 1981–3
Golf 1 GL 1.5 1981–3
Golf 1 GLS 1.5 1977–81
Golf 1 GLS 1.3 1979–81
Golf 1 Convertible GL 1.3 1984–5

Golf 1 Convertible GLS 1.5 1979–81
Golf 1 Convertible GL 1.5 1981–3
Golf 1 Convertible GL 1.6 1983–9
Golf 1 Convertible GL 1.8 1983–9
Golf 1 Convertible GLI 1.6 1979–82
Golf 1 Convertible GLI 1.8 1982–9
Golf 1 Cabriolet 1.8 1989–on
Golf 1 Convertible GTI 1.8 1989–on
Jetta 1 1.3 1979–82
Jetta 1 C 1.3 1982–3
Jetta 1 C 1.5 1982–3
Jetta 1 C, CL & GL Diesel 1.6 1982–3
Jetta 1 C, CL & GL Turbodiesel
  1.6 1982–3
Jetta 1 L 1.3 1979–82
Jetta 1 CL 1.3 1982–3
Jetta 1 CL 1.5 1982–3
Jetta 1 CL 1,6 1982–3
Jetta 1 GL 1.3 1979–82
Jetta 1 GL 1.5 1982–3
Jetta 1 GL 1.6 1982–3
Jetta 1 S 1.5 1979–82
Jetta 1 LS 1.5 1979–82
Jetta 1 GLS 1.5 1979–82
Jetta 1 Li 1.6 1979–81
Jetta 1 CLi 1.6 1982
Jetta 1 CLi 1.8 1982–3

Jetta 1 GLi 1.6 1979–82
Jetta 1 GLi 1.8 1982–3
Scirocco 1 1.1 1974–9
Scirocco 1 1.3 1979–81
Scirocco 1 L 1.1 1974–9
Scirocco 1 L 1.3 1979–81
Scirocco 1 S 1.6 1977, 1978–81
Scirocco 1 S 1.5 1977–81
Scirocco 1 LS 1.5 1974–5, 1977–81
Scirocco 1 TS 1.5 1974–5
Scirocco 1 LS 1.6 1975–7, 1978–81
Scirocco 1 TS 1.6 1975–6
Scirocco 1 GT 1.6 1976–7, 1978–81
Scirocco 1 GT 1.5 1977–81
Scirocco 1 GT 1.3 1979–81
Scirocco 1 GL 1.6 1976–7, 1978–81
Scirocco 1 GL 1.5 1977–81
Scirocco 1 GTi 1.6 1976–81
Scirocco 1 GLi 1.6 1976–81
Golf 2 C 1.3 1983–7
Golf 2 C 1.6 1983–7
Golf 2 C 1.8 1983–7
Golf 2 1.3 1987–9
Golf 2 1.6 1987–9
Golf 2 1.8 1987–9
Golf 2 CL 1.3 1983–91
Golf 2 CL 1.6 1983–91

Golf 2 GL 1.3 1983–91
Golf 2 GL 1.6 1983–91
Golf 2 GL 1.8 1983–91
Golf 2 Carat 1.8 1983–6
Golf 2 GT 1.8 1987–91
Golf 2 GTI 1.8 1983–91
Golf 2 GTI 16V 1.8 1985–91
Golf 2 GTI G60 1.8 1989–91
Golf 2 C Diesel 1.6 1983–89
Golf 2 CL & GL Diesel 1.6 1983–91
Golf 2 CL, GL & GTD Turbodiesel
   1983–91
Golf 2 Syncro CL & GT 1.8 1986–8
Golf 2 Country 1.8 1989–91
Jetta 2 C 1.3 1983–6
Jetta 2 C 1.6 1983–6
Jetta 2 C 1.8 1983–6
Jetta 2 1.3 1986–8
Jetta 2 1.6 1986–8
Jetta 2 1.8 1986–8
Jetta 2 CL 1.3 1983–91
Jetta 2 CL 1.6 1983–91
Jetta 2 CL 1.8 1983–91
Jetta 2 GL 1.3 1983–91

Jetta 2 GL 1.6 1983–91
Jetta 2 GL 1.8 1983–91
Jetta 2 Carat 1.8 1983–9
Jetta 2 C Diesel 1.6 1983–7
Jetta 2 CL & GL Diesel 1.6 1983–91
Jetta 2 C Turbo Diesel 1.6 1983–7
Jetta 2 CL, GL and GT Turbodiesel
   1983–91
Jetta 2 GT & GTi 1.8 1984–91
Jetta 2 GT & GTi 16V 1.8 1987–91
Jetta 2 TX 1.6 1986–91
Jetta 2 GTX 1.8 1987–8
Jetta 2 GTX 16V 1.8 1988
Jetta 2 GL & GT Syncro 1.8 1988–91
Scirocco 2 L 1.3 1981–2
Scirocco 2 GL 1.3 1981–4
Scirocco 2 LS 1.5 1981–2
Scirocco 2 LS 1.6 1981–2
Scirocco 2 CL 1.3 1982–5
Scirocco 2 CL 1.5 1982–3
Scirocco 2 CL 1.6 1982–5
Scirocco 2 CL 1.8 1984–5
Scirocco 2 GL 1.5 1981–3
Scirocco 2 GL 1.6 1981–5

Scirocco 2 GL 1.8 1984–5
Scirocco 2 GT 1.3 1983–4
Scirocco 2 GT 1.5 1981–3
Scirocco 2 GT 1.6 1981–8
Scirocco 2 GT 1.8 1984–9
Scirocco 2 GT II 1.8 1989–92
Scirocco 2 GT 16V 1.8 1985–8
Scirocco 2 GTL 1.6 1985–7
Scirocco 2 GTL 1.8 1985–7
Scirocco 2 GTi 1.6 1981–2
Scirocco 2 GTi 1.8 1982–4
Scirocco 2 GLi 1.6 1981–2
Scirocco 2 GLi 1.8 1982–4
Scirocco 2 16V 1.8 1984–5
Scirocco 2 GTX 1.6 1984–6
Scirocco 2 GTX 1.8 1984–8
Scirocco 2 GTX 16V 1.8 1985–8
Scirocco 2 Scala 1.8 1989–92
Corrado 16V 1.8 1989–1991
Corrado 16V 2.0 1991–on
Corrado G60 1.8 1989–on
Corrado VR6 2.9 1992–on

APPENDIX D

Performance figures for high-performance Golfs and derivatives

In keeping with the policy established with the first *Collector's Guide* in 1978 and maintained ever since, the author has sought the most highly respected source for accurate performance figures, namely the weekly journals *Autocar* and *Motor*, whose names are now united in the title of one magazine, to the editor of which grateful thanks are extended.

Model	GOLF 1 GLS	GOLF 1 GTI	GOLF 1 GTI	GOLF 2 GTI	GOLF 2 GTI 16V	GOLF 2 GL	JETTA GLi	JETTA GTi 16V
Engine capacity (cc)	1272	1588	1781	1781	1781	1595	1588	1781
Maximum power (bhp)	60	110	112	112	139	75	110	139
Mean maximum speed (mph)	95	112	118	119	123	104	112	128
Acceleration (sec)								
0–30mph	4.0	3.3	3.0	3.0	2.7	3.7	3.0	3.1
0–40mph	6.1	4.9	4.3	4.3	4.2	5.6	4.4	4.5
0–50mph	9.1	7.0	5.9	6.1	5.9	8.0	6.2	6.0
0–60mph	13.2	9.6	8.1	8.3	8.0	11.6	8.6	7.7
0–70mph	18.6	13.0	10.6	11.0	10.9	16.2	11.2	10.3
0–80mph	29.0	17.0	15.0	14.4	13.5	22.7	15.0	13.1
0–90mph	–	22.7	19.6	18.5	18.1	33.9	20.3	17.0
0–100mph	–	35.3	28.8	26.6	23.3	–	30.0	22.5
Standing ¼-mile (sec)	18.9	17.2	16.2	16.5	16.2	18.3	16.3	16.2
Top gear acceleration (sec)								
20–40mph	11.0	10.5	9.7	8.8	9.4	10.5	10.6	10.7
30–50mph	10.1	9.8	9.1	8.3	9.1	9.9	9.3	10.4
40–60mph	11.2	9.8	8.9	8.0	9.2	10.8	9.4	10.5
50–70mph	13.0	10.5	9.1	8.2	9.5	12.2	9.7	11.5
60–80mph	17.9	12.1	11.2	9.1	10.4	14.5	11.4	13.5
70–90mph	–	14.6	13.2	11.1	11.7	20.7	14.2	–
80–100mph	–	–	15.8	13.8	13.9	–	–	–
Overall fuel consumption (mpg)	29.3	28.5	28.8	30.6	25.3	32.7	26.9	30.1
Test weight (lb)	2173	2228	2261	2420	2456	2440	2352	2843
Tested by	*Motor*	*Motor*	*Motor*	*Motor*	*A/car*	*Motor*	*Motor*	*Motor*
Test published	12/79	12/76	11/82	5/84	5/86	2/84	4/80	1/88

Model	SCIROCCO GLS	SCIROCCO GTi	SCIROCCO GTX	SCIROCCO GTX 16V	CORRADO 16V	CORRADO 16V	CORRADO G60	CORRADO VR6
Engine capacity (cc)	1588	1588	1781	1781	1781	1984	1781	2861
Maximum power (bhp)	85	110	112	139	136	136	160	190
Mean maximum speed (mph)	101	115	117	130	131	126	137	144
Acceleration (sec)								
0–30mph	3.8	3.3	3.1	3.1	3.1	3.6	3.0	2.6
0–40mph	5.6	5.2	4.9	4.4	4.7	5.4	4.7	3.8
0–50mph	8.1	7.2	6.6	6.0	6.4	7.5	6.4	5.4
0–60mph	11.5	9.8	9.4	7.8	8.7	10.2	8.9	7.2
0–70mph	15.7	12.9	12.2	10.4	11.4	13.4	11.8	9.5
0–80mph	21.8	16.7	16.2	13.2	14.5	17.4	14.5	12.0
0–90mph	34.0	21.8	21.7	16.9	18.7	22.9	19.1	15.2
0–100mph	–	32.2	30.8	22.1	23.9	30.4	24.0	19.2
Standing ¼–mile (sec)	17.7	17.6	17.1	16.2	16.5	17.8	16.8	15.6
Top gear acceleration (sec)								
20–40mph	10.9	11.0	9.6	10.2	12.4	11.6	12.5	9.8
30–50mph	9.3	10.4	9.3	10.1	12.2	10.9	10.4	9.4
40–60mph	9.9	10.2	9.1	9.5	11.8	11.2	10.0	9.5
50–70mph	11.5	10.4	9.5	10.1	12.1	11.6	9.6	9.6
60–80mph	13.2	12.2	11.0	11.7	13.4	12.3	9.6	9.9
70–90mph	–	15.0	13.2	12.9	14.8	13.4	10.2	10.4
80–100mph	–	–	–	14.9	16.5	15.7	11.3	10.7
Overall fuel consumption (mpg)	25.1	29.1	30.4	27.6	29.5	31.3	22.0	24.9
Test weight (lb)	2184	2440	2517	2535	2939	2614	2903	2733
Tested by	*Motor*	*Motor*	*Motor*	*Motor*	*Acar&M*	*Acar&M*	*Acar&M*	*Acar&M*
Test published	2/77	2/82	12/84	5/86	5/89	7/92	10/90	4/92